The
GLENEAGLES
Hotel

The GLENEAGLES *Hotel*

75 YEARS *of* SCOTTISH EXCELLENCE

JANE NOTTAGE

HarperCollins*Illustrated*
London

To Benedict, whom I love and miss very much

I would like to thank my parents, Geoffrey and Margaret, who sustain me through the hard times and help me celebrate the good; Roger Kelly, who researched and wrote the golf section in the book; all my family and friends, and everyone at The Gleneagles Hotel, especially Peter Lederer, known as the 'whirlwind' for his endless energy, Terry Waldron, who has dedicated many hours to pulling the book together, likewise Margaret Ellis, and Mike Picken, who created and supervised the recipes. At HarperCollins I would like to thank especially my patient and talented editors, Barbara Dixon and Fiona Screen, and Fiona Wilson of Cameron Wilson for being a friend as well as a business associate; Arthur Brown for his wonderful design, Graham Lees for the great photography, and Home Economist Wendy Barrie. Many thanks also to my agent, the master negotiator Jonathan Lloyd of Curtis Brown.

The Hotel wishes to thank all guests and employees, past and present, who have contributed to this book. Thanks also to United Distillers and Vintners, Lex Land Rover and Highland Spring.

First published in 1999 by
HarperCollins*Illustrated*,
an imprint of
HarperCollins*Publishers*
77-85 Fulham Palace Road
London W6 8JB

The HarperCollins website address is:
www.**fire**and**water**.com

Text © Jane Nottage 1999
Photographs pages 11, 13tr, 13bl, 14, 16, 19, 20, 21, 22, 24, 25, 26, 27, 28, 29, 51, 58, 62, 85, 87, 88, 89b, 91, 92, 93, 94, 95, 97, 99, 102, 105, 109, 117, 118, 132, 143, 144, 145, 147, 150, 151, 152, 153, 159, 161, 166, 169, 173, 177, 178b, 179, 181, 184 © HarperCollins*Publishers* 1999
Photographs pages 1, 2, 5, 8, 13tl, 13bl, 17, 18, 30, 32, 33, 35, 36, 39, 40, 41, 42, 43, 44, 46, 55, 56, 59, 61, 68t, 71, 72, 74, 76, 81, 89t, 110, 111, 114, 115, 121, 122, 125, 126, 128, 130, 135, 137, 148, 155, 157, 158, 163, 167, 168, 171, 174, 175, 178t, 180, 182, 185, 186, 187 © Gleneagles Hotel 1999
Photographs pages 78, 140 © Russell Kirk 1999

Jane Nottage reserves the moral right to be identified as the author of this work

A CIP catalogue record for this book is available from the British Library

ISBN: 000 414061 3

Design: Arthur Brown
Food Photography: Graham Lees
Home Economist: Wendy Barrie
Index: Susan Bosanko

99 01 03 02 00
2 4 6 8 9 7 5 3 1

Colour reproduction by Colourscan Pte. ltd
Printed and bound in Italy

Contents

FOREWORD

by JACKIE STEWART

The Gleneagles Hotel has always held very special memories for me. When I was a boy I remember going for lunch and afternoon tea with my father and feeling cosseted and cared for in this grand and luxurious place. At that time it was a highly exclusive retreat for the leisured classes to enjoy their summer vacations, playing golf and indulging in the activities that were characteristic of that era.

However, over the years the hotel has evolved from being not only a golf centre but one of the best international leisure resorts in the world. There is something for everyone at Gleneagles – golf, shooting, falconry or equestrian activities for the energetic, or the more gentle pursuits found in the Spa and The Club for those who simply want to relax.

And then there's the famed Scottish hospitality. As a Scot, I am biased, but I truly believe there is nowhere more welcoming than Scotland. I always look forward to coming home, knowing that my heart will be warmed and spirit soothed as I take a break from the demands of daily life. The feeling that nothing is too much trouble for the Scots is both relaxing and energising, and it fills me with new ideas and plans.

Being the grandson of a gamekeeper, and having shot for Scotland and Great Britain in clay target shooting before becoming a racing driver, I am immensely proud to be associated with The Gleneagles Hotel through the Jackie Stewart Shooting and Fishing schools. These schools are the fruit of the rapport I feel with the place that has become my second home. Gleneagles and I have grown together and shared many happy moments. The last Rolex/Jackie Stewart Celebrity Challenge, for example, raised over £650,000 for charity and over the years in this event we have enjoyed wonderful days in the company of the Princess Royal, the Duke of York, Prince Edward, the late King Hussein and the Queen Noor of Jordan, the King and Queen of Greece, HRH The Duke of Kent and such well-known personalities as Dame Kiri Te Kanawa, Sean Connery, Steven Spielberg, Harrison Ford and celebrities from every field.

I have also spent some wonderful family times at The Gleneagles Hotel with my wife Helen, my children Paul and Mark, and, more recently, with my sons' own wives and families. We will all be at the hotel to celebrate the new millennium, which I am sure will be an unforgettable experience. Peter Lederer and his management team have maintained the reputation of excellence and hospitality that the hotel is known for throughout the world, and I know that they all embrace the 21st century with hope and enthusiasm.

It is a pleasure for me to be associated with this book, which celebrates the history and unique style of somewhere that has a very special place in my heart. I hope you will come and visit The Gleneagles Hotel and experience the warmth and hospitality of my homeland. For me the hotel is more than a place of rest and replenishment; it has become my lifelong friend, and I am sure it will become yours.

The Highland Palace

Bonnie Charlie's noo awa,
Safely o'er the friendly main;
Mony a heart will break in twa,
Should he ne'er come back again.
Will ye no come back again?
Will ye no come back again?

*T*HE GLENEAGLES HOTEL was officially opened on the 7th of June 1924, although it was first conceived fourteen years previously. In fact, nature determined long ago that this beautiful area would become a Highland mecca providing spiritual and physical refreshment for the weary traveller.

The rolling hills which form a romantic and protective circle around this magnificent jewel in the Highland crown, and upon which the sun and moon form dancing images of light and shadow, were formed about 350 million years ago from hard volcanic rocks and deposits of glacial origin. If we have the gods, then, to thank for their benevolent disposition in creating a place of such natural beauty, we have one man to thank for his ability to transform a romantic dream into the beautiful hotel that graces the Highlands today.

In 1910, Donald Matheson, General Manager of the Caledonian Railway Company, was relaxing on holiday in the Strathearn valley – the area in which Gleneagles sits. It was the first moment he had been able to look around the stunning landscape and for several days he was bewitched by the magical splendour of the land. As he stood there in contemplation, he realised that it was the ideal place to build a 'Grand Hotel', a place that would provide first-class hospitality and golf facilities for the leisured classes.

A man with a visionary and pioneering spirit, Donald Matheson was not just driven by romanticism, but was a hard-headed businessman who wanted to be the best and outdo the competition to capture the ever-expanding leisure market.

OPPOSITE:
LAICH LOCH
Stunning views bear
testimony to the care and
dedication of the gardeners
and groundsmen of The
Gleneagles Hotel.

AUCHTERARDER – SITE *of the* GLENEAGLES HOTEL

*A*S DONALD MATHESON stood on the site chosen for The Gleneagles Hotel, which was known as the White Muir of Auchterarder, his imagination would have leapt back several centuries to the great historical events that had taken place in the area.

The small town of Auchterarder has played a key role in some of the most important events of Scottish history. It lies in the Ochil Hills, halfway between the historical cities of Perth and Stirling, at the foot of the humpbacked formation, Craig Rossie. The foothills of the Grampian mountain chain form a barrier to the north and on a clear day you can see the distinctive outline of Ben Lomond to the west, and to the east the sea, 40 miles down the strath. Stirling, as the gateway to the Highlands, is a city of great military significance and Perth, with its ancient royal palace of Scone, is the place where Scottish kings were traditionally crowned.

According to Celtic legend, the Stone of Scone travelled from The Holy Land to Ireland, where in 700 BC it was placed on the Hills of Tara, the ancient crowning-place of the kings of Ireland. It was captured by Celtic Scottish invaders and in 840 AD brought to the village of Scone and encased in the royal coronation chair. However, Edward I of England snatched it away and took it to his homeland. He too built a coronation chair under which the Stone was placed. Finally, on St Andrew's Day 1996, the Stone was restored to Scotland, this time by peaceful rather than violent means.

In 1745, the galloping hooves of invading horses could be heard when Charles Stuart, or Bonnie Prince Charlie, as he was more affectionately known, decided to return to Scotland from exile in France and declare himself King of Scotland and of England. On the 12th of September 1745 Charles stopped at Auchterarder and held a review of his army in a bid to encourage others from the area to unite with them in their fight to return Catholicism to the English throne. Refreshed by his stay in Auchterarder, the dashing prince, full of hope and in high spirits, set off to conquer England. Unfortunately, he soon lost the scent of victory and, suffering poor support from the French and English, was heavily defeated by the Duke of Cumberland at the disastrous battle of Culloden Moor in 1746. The prince held a historic summit in Crieff, which is situated just down the glen from Auchterarder, and it is here that it was decided that he and the Scottish regiments should 'take the high road' to Inverness, while the horses and low country regiments took the 'low road' via the coast to the same destination.

BONNIE PRINCE CHARLIE

Bonnie Prince Charlie's army was effectively wiped out at this famous battle and he was forced to flee back to France and exile.

How different it might have been if Bonnie Prince Charlie had been able to rest awhile in the splendour of The Gleneagles Hotel! Would his spirits have been restored? Would his troops have stayed with him? Could the course of history have been changed and the battle of Culloden won? If Charles Stuart had reigned, then Charles Windsor would not be the current heir to the British throne and his mother, Queen Elizabeth II, would not be Queen today.

The present Royal Family enjoys the hallowed peace and protection of The Gleneagles Hotel and I believe that Princess Anne would still visit to ride, shoot and relax, even if she were not part of the ruling monarchy. Similarly, the Queen's second son, Prince Andrew, a talented golf player, would no doubt still be drawn to this Scottish palace to test his skill on the championship courses. Yet as the Windsors enjoy the hospitality of The Gleneagles Hotel, it is strange to think that they are walking the same turf that over two hundred years ago nearly changed their destiny.

His great grandson, Nigel Kenyon, explains Mr Matheson's philosophy: 'He had a belief that if you had the traveller in your pocket on the train, you might as well keep him in your pocket when he finished his journey. He oversaw the development of city-based hotels to provide the businessman with accommodation and he thought the next step was to provide the holiday traveller with hotels that would meet his leisure needs.'

Immersed in history, cloaked in legend and offering the guest a protective luxury, The Gleneagles Hotel has become a world-famous landmark. It has survived two world wars (the first one halted its construction) and fought off the cruel winds of recession. Like the ever-changing colours of the Ochil Hills that surround it, Gleneagles has a chameleon quality that has enabled it to respond to the needs of a society changed beyond all recognition from the heady, socialite whirl of the 1920s and 1930s. It has evolved into one of the truly great modern resort hotels, where businessmen and golfers can bring their families, safe in the knowledge that there is plenty of entertainment available for everyone.

A HOME FROM HOME

11

I first stayed at the hotel in January 1995. I was writing a book and I wanted somewhere quiet to work, away from the distractions of London. Gleneagles became a home from home – luxurious but protective. Whatever I needed was laid on. I stayed for three weeks and saw at first hand what it is like to be a part of The Gleneagles Experience. The chef came to have a chat about what type of food I liked and my favourite peppermint tea bags were put in the room, as were endless bars of KitKats, which I could then work off in the gym, where my personal instructors would help me achieve my fitness targets. The staff look upon their guests as part of a large, constantly evolving family – I discovered I was not simply a visitor in an anonymous hotel, but a guest in a private house.

SENTRIES OF STONE
Around the main building of the hotel stone eagles keep silent vigil over the manicured lawns.

As Lt Colonel Ron Smith, the former Guest Services Manager (see page 120), told me, 'We have two objectives at Gleneagles. The first is to make every guest who walks through the front door think they're the most important person that has come in here today, and to leave thinking that, and the second objective is to surpass the expectations that every guest has of Gleneagles.'

Like the Stone of Scone, or the dreams of Bonnie Prince Charlie, there is a certain mysticism about Gleneagles which means the sum of its parts creates something greater than each individual component. As general managers change, somehow this mysticism is carried through, and the legend lives on. Looking to the future, plans are well in hand for the millennium celebrations, and the hotel has its own vision of how it will respond to the demands of the 21st century.

The principles and ideology that first motivated Donald Matheson when he conceived this great 'Highland Palace' are the same ones that govern Gleneagles today. The glory of the hotel will continue to thrill and delight its guests and the staff who have become part of the Gleneagles family. This book is a celebration of The Gleneagles Hotel through the eyes of the families and friends who have worked at, visited and grown to love the 'Scottish playground'.

CHAPTER ONE

The Sum of the Parts

I saw a stranger yestreen;
I put food in the eating place;
Drink in the drinking place;
Music in the listening place;
In the sacred name of the Triune;
He blessed myself and my house.

FROM 'RUNE OF HOSPITALITY'
TRADITIONAL

12

OPPOSITE:
A DAY IN THE LIFE
Early morning guests
(top left) chat in the
lobby of the hotel.
Executive Head Chef
Mike Picken and Premier
Sous Chef Andy Hamer
(top right) discuss future
menus. For some, the day
simply has to begin with a
round of golf (bottom
right) while for others a
session of aqua aerobics
(bottom left) helps to
rejuvenate tired bodies.

IFE AT GLENEAGLES ebbs and flows in tune with the rhythm of the human race itself. There is a constant hum of activity throughout the hotel. Business delegates arrive, set up exhibitions, discuss strategy and future plans, pack up and go on their way again. Golfers come to play the best round of their lives and relive it afterwards in the bars and restaurants. Families, lovers, friends, relations flow in and out, all with their own hopes, dreams and expectations of what it will be like to stay at The Gleneagles Hotel.

In the banqueting rooms weddings, anniversaries and birthdays are celebrated, while in The Strathearn Restaurant guests plan their futures over a romantic dinner. Gleneagles witnesses a host of changing moods, feelings and expectations every day. Some people are in serious business mode, expecting to discuss strategy and make important decisions, some are in romantic and reflective mood as they arrive to celebrate an anniversary, and some are feeling active, ready to compete in a few rounds of golf or put in some mileage before breakfast, jogging around the stunning hotel grounds. Responding to all these hopes and expectations are the staff, who manage to weave the dreams into a tangible reality.

The weaving of dreams might look easy, but it isn't. A hotel with over 200 rooms, 3 restaurants and The Bar, a ballroom, a boardroom, several custom-built conference suites, 10 private function rooms, three 18-hole championship golf courses, a clubhouse, a golf shop, a 9-hole 'Wee Course', a golf academy, a

14

VISUAL SPLENDOUR
As day dawns at The Gleneagles Hotel the beauty of the surrounding landscape comes to life.

leisure club, a spa, an equestrian centre, a falconry school, a shooting school, a garden centre, 4 all-weather tennis courts, 1 grass court, 2 salmon and sea trout angling beats on the River Tay, lochs for brown trout, off road driving facilities, lawn bowls, croquet, pitch and putt, jogging trails and shops takes a lot of managing, and first-class co-ordination.

Each department works to its own rhythm, but is always aware that it must fit into the overall functioning of the hotel. A lot can happen in 24 hours, and usually does! From the kitchens to the bedrooms, from the public rooms to the reception area, each place has its own special life.

A DAY IN THE LIFE OF THE GLENEAGLES HOTEL

3.30 am All is quiet as Breakfast Chef Norman Brockie drives into the staff car park at the back of the hotel and parks near the entrance to the kitchen. It is still dark and he pauses for a moment to draw breath and enjoy a little peace before the hustle and bustle commences. In just over three hours' time, The Strathearn Restaurant will open for breakfast and there could be as many as 500 people to impress with one of the finest and most comprehensive breakfasts in the world. Norman shuts the door of his car and enters his kingdom. 'It's brilliant,' he says, 'really quiet. There's no-one around except the cleaners so I can get on with my work in peace.'

As well as catering for several hundred guests for breakfast, Norman must oversee the room service orders. There's not much time during the next eight hours to snatch a few quiet moments.

Norman might feel as if he's alone when he arrives but the truth is quite the opposite. Night Chef Carlton Doudney is already hard at work preparing breakfasts and cooking for anyone who might fancy some kippers and bacon in the middle of the night.

In The Bar, Barman Magnus Heron and his colleagues are just getting to the end of a long day. The serious *après*-dinner drinkers, usually the conference attendees, are just about to call it a day and wander off to bed.

4.00 am Norman, resplendent in his chef's whites, officially starts work. First on the agenda is the preparation of the porridge. He makes two kinds of porridge, a traditional one made with water and a very special version made with milk and served with whipped cream, seasonal berries soaked in Drambuie and a sprinkling of toasted oatmeal – definitely not one for guests counting the calories.

The porridge needs a slow, 3-hour cook, so Norman has to assemble the ingredients, which these days he can judge without weighing, and put the saucepans on to simmer.

4.00 am In the front office the computers have just come back on line after having completed their night audit. Now the early morning bills can be prepared.

4.15 am Most of the guests are still asleep, but the kitchen is buzzing. The porridge is cooking and Norman starts on the bacon and sausages. He starts to cook the bacon (guests are offered two types – streaky or back) and the sausages, and then cooks the mushrooms.

4.30 am In the summer, the first groups (generally the Americans) are checking out by this time, ready to move on to their next destination. The Americans are often the last to arrive and the first to leave, necessarily so given the punishing schedules they set themselves, in a bid to fit in all the sights and play on all the great golf courses in Europe. Before they leave they enjoy a continental-style breakfast and a much-needed coffee to keep them awake.

5.00 am Norman takes a break and enjoys his last moment of peace and quiet. Soon the waiters and receptionists, porters and housekeepers will be arriving to make sure everything is shipshape for the guests. Norman has a companion to chat to during his break: Max, the Night Manager, is eating a bowl of Rice Krispies and mulling over the night's dramas.

6.15 am Santo Bruno, the Head Breakfast Waiter, arrives for work and discusses breakfast arrangements with Norman, who is in overall charge.

PROVISIONS FOR BREAKFAST
(for 450 people)

48 dozen eggs

40 lb bacon

10 lb tomatoes

20 lb mushrooms

25 loaves white bread

25 loaves brown bread

4 dozen large crumpets

4 dozen waffles

4 dozen potato scones

18 dozen small round potato scones

8 dozen large potato scones

15

NORMAN BROCKIE – THE PORRIDGE MASTER

*E*VERY WEEK Norman gets through 56 lb of pure pinhead oatmeal from Perth to make 2 gallons of Scottish traditional porridge and 1½ gallons of creamy porridge every day.

Norman is really rather good at making porridge. In fact, he has been crowned World Porridge Champion, winning the award in 1995. Norman's love for porridge stems from his childhood. 'My auntie used to go into the byre in the morning and milk the cows. She would sit on a milking stool, resting her forehead against the cow, and collect the milk in a 2-gallon stainless steel container. Meanwhile, the porridge would have been cooking all night and we'd dunk our thick porridge in the milk. It was delicious – a taste that remains part of my childhood.'

6.30 am Norman's day is coming to a crescendo as the bacon, sausages, tomatoes and potatoes are all cooked and placed on hot plates. The breakfast waiters have arrived and are putting the milk and sugar out on the trays and setting up the buffet tables.

6.50 am The hot food is removed from the hot plates and taken to The Strathearn Restaurant.

6.55 am The chambermaids, or house assistants, as they are now known, are in full swing, changing beds, cleaning, polishing and replenishing the complimentary coffee, tea and shortbread that welcome the guests in every room. Like painting the Forth Road Bridge, this is a task that is never finished. Guests arrive, leave, sleep in, check out late, require extra towels, pillows or blankets. Sheila Perera is the highly efficient Executive Housekeeper. Under her jurisdiction, the housekeeping department has now moved from a tiny office on the second floor to the main back corridor. 'Housekeeping is at the heart of the hotel,' explains Sheila. 'Everyone knows where we are and they come to us for anything they need. We supply a needle, a thread, and sympathy.'

Sheila is a new-style manager and has trained her house assistants to check their own work so they can be confident that the rooms can be booked for a new guest without any need for re-checking. Pride in your work is of paramount importance and is part of the Gleneagles philosophy of offering the best service to the guests at all times.

Sheila is also in charge of room service. Guests' room service requirements tend to reach their peak around 7.00 am. People are asking for breakfasts, drinks, valet service or extra towels and clothes pressed. Then there are the honeymooners in room 142 who have just ordered fillet steaks and champagne for breakfast!

7.00 am By now, the finest breakfast in the world is under way in The Strathearn Restaurant. A veritable morning feast greets the first guests. Assorted juices from apple to elderflower, sparkling water, breakfast cereals and muesli, yoghurts, fresh fruit from five continents, cheeses, stone-baked Scottish rolls and Danish pastries. And that's just on one table. From the centre table guests can feast on Norman's famous traditional and 'special' porridges, pork and herb link sausages, grilled trout fillet, scrambled eggs and smoked Tay salmon, free-range eggs cooked any way you want them, grilled tomatoes, field mushrooms, home-cured bacon and potato scones, lemon pancakes

with streaky bacon and Drambuie-flavoured waffles with maple syrup. If that doesn't satisfy your appetite then try the *à la carte* 'cooked to order' alternatives. Poached Finnan haddock, Loch Fyne kippers with melted butter, black pudding, cloutie dumpling with vegetarian sausages and home-made baked beans on toast.

Looking for something special to drink? Then why not try a herbal tea, hot chocolate, cappuccino or The Gleneagles Frothy (a coffee with plenty of froth and a delicate taste of chocolate). Full up? Well, you could always try the haggis, which features on the breakfast menu twice a week. Now are you ready for your morning's activities?

7.00 am If you feel a little exercise might be in order before breakfast, then The Club is open and manager Claire Birchall is awaiting your arrival. At 7.00 am the first guests arrive for an early-morning swim or an hour's work-out in the state-of-the-art Technogym. The Club members are usually quick off the mark, followed by the most enthusiastic guests.

The Club was transformed in 1998, courtesy of a £2.7 million facelift, and is now a truly world-class facility able to offer a wide range of sporting and leisure activities to suit every taste and age group. A new lap pool means that keen swimmers are able to do their circuits without interruption, while the Jacuzzi, the 'volcano' feature of the smaller pool and the outdoor hot pool provide hours of fun for the kids or older members who are still young at heart.

LINEN TALLY *(per year)*

80,000 sheets
100,000 bath towels
131,000 hand towels
58,000 soap bars
20,000 toilet rolls

CONSTANT CARE
The house assistants in action at the start of another busy day.

7.00 am Eileen Kenyon, one of the front of house managers, arrives for work. She shares shifts with her colleagues Kerry McKenzie and Pamela McGowan. The front of house managers, who work as duty managers, have control of the reception and concierge areas, as well as resort sales. Eileen picks up the bleep and the set of master keys and takes over from Night Manager Max, who is just about to clock off duty.

Eileen has to liaise with the head of the shift on Reception to see if there are any problems to sort out, or any special requirements to attend to, such as organising a separate check-in for groups of guests arriving that day. Then there are the more unusual requests – one Christmas Eve a lady guest asked for a breast pump and the staff had to go all the way to Edinburgh to find one and bring it back to the hotel for her. She was very happy with the pump as it allowed her to participate in the season's parties.

OPPOSITE:
THE RECEPTION
Staff prepare for rush hour at the reception desk.

Eileen checks the VIP list to see which important personalities will be arriving, and looks up their guest history. Some VIPs like a full bar, others like certain whiskies and some like fruit or chocolates. Whatever the individual preferences, the important thing is to make sure everyone, VIP or not, receives a special welcome.

The rooms are checked and flowers arranged. Master cake and pastry creator Ian Ironside's 'marzipan whisky men' are lovingly placed in some of the rooms. If there is a chauffeur pick-up at the airport or railway station Eileen makes sure the chauffeur has the correct pick-up time. The chauffeur then rings the hotel when the car is about five or ten minutes away so that the guests can be welcomed at the front door and escorted straight up to their room. Eileen does her utmost to ensure that guests are allocated the same room each time they return to the hotel.

7.00 am As the guests are tucking into their morning feast, Tom Watson, the starter on The King's Course, is arriving for work. Six years ago, Tom retired from a lifetime devoted to farming. Within six months Tom had found the dream retirement occupation for an insatiable golf enthusiast. Now he spends five days a week, from 7.00 am to 3.45 pm, making sure that everyone tees off on time and in the best possible frame of mind to enjoy a game on one of the world's finest golf courses.

When he arrives Tom looks at the list of people playing on The King's that day and checks their tee-off times. Then he settles down in his stylish, white 'house' with its stunning white Rolex clock on top and awaits his first customer. Come rain or shine, Tom can guarantee the first golfers will soon be making their way towards him.

18

ONE UP *on the* COMPETITION

NORMAN and his staff have done a bit of research and he knows perfectly well how to avoid the mistakes of his competitors. 'Cold, congealed food is the most usual mistake,' he says. 'A group of us went round to our main competitors' hotels and tried out their breakfasts. Not only were we pleased with our own, but we discovered that a lot of breakfasts were served up in a pretty sorry state, with cold plates and, as a result, cold food.'

At Gleneagles the chefs make sure the food doesn't go cold by having pans with four heating gels underneath to keep the water boiling and the food hot. With the result that the Gleneagles breakfast is one of the best breakfasts you will ever eat.

7.00 am Peter Lederer, Managing Director of The
Gleneagles Hotel, arrives in London for his first
meeting of the day. One of the topics for discussion is
the hotel industry's scholarships. Peter is known as 'the
whirlwind' and has been up since just after Norman
Brockie started to cook breakfast. Peter will be on the
go until well after Max arrives to start his shift. 'O
Lord! Thou knowest how busy I must be this day: if I
forget thee, do not thou forget me.' The prayer recited
before the battle of Edgehill could have been created
especially for Peter Lederer.

7.30 am The really eager golfers are at the first tee and
Tom Watson is greeting, organising and encouraging.
'Our golfers come from all over the world. They bring
great expectations and many are nervous of playing on
The King's Course. I always have a wee chat with
them, calm them down and get them in the right frame of mind to do themselves
justice,' he says. 'There were two ladies from Ohio who were very nervous about
playing on The King's, and I just said, "Come on ladies, this course is a piece of
cake," and off they went, full of vigour and determination.'

PETER LEDERER

19

One of Tom's responsibilities is to advise on the weather and he listens to the
local forecast on Radio Scotland as he drives into work in the morning. 'If it looks
like a very wet day, I'll usually say, "you should be finished before it rains," and
hopefully they will be. It's important to remain optimistic when it comes to the
forces of nature.'

RICHARD CANNON

Tom is often asked to take photos for golfers who want a
memento of the day.

7.30 am As Tom is seeing off the early golfers Richard
Cannon, one of the caddies, is also commencing the first job of
his very busy day. A lot of guests keep to the same caddy and
book him or her when they book their round of golf. A caddy
can make or break your day. Many golfers are unused to the
winds and if left to their own devices will hit the ball short.
Richard sees his job as 'motivating and cheering them up
when things go wrong'. Richard knows the Gleneagles golf
courses inside out. He can give expert advice on which club to
use for which shot, where to aim for, how to compensate for
the weather conditions and, most importantly, how to get out
of the rough.

Richard will be hoping that the guests who come out on
the Gleneagles courses for a game today will want to play on
his favourite course – The Queen's Course. The Queen's is not
as difficult a course as The King's, so there's not so much to

carry, but it is more subtle and has intricacies that players need to be made aware of. It calls for greater precision and that means more interesting work for the caddy.

7.45 am Back in the hotel, Norman, our intrepid breakfast chef, is not only cooking the *à la carte* orders, but preparing room service breakfasts as well. As he explains, some people's demands know no bounds: 'We had a room service card put outside one of the rooms and they requested absolutely everything – kippers, haddock, cloutie dumpling, poached eggs, fried eggs, scrambled eggs, sausages, bacon and black pudding. In the end we sent up six plates for just two people.' Sumo wrestlers, or a honeymoon couple, or maybe a combination of both.

From the room service menu guests can choose the Monarch's breakfast, which is just as it sounds – a breakfast fit for a king. Along with your half bottle of champagne you have a choice of chilled fruit juice, a compote of prunes, apricots, figs and berries in season, smoked salmon and scrambled eggs or sirloin of Angus beef, two poached eggs, bacon, sausage, tomatoes and mushrooms and a basket of freshly baked rolls, croissants and Danish pastries.

HEATHER EDMENT
at the Dormy Clubhouse
discussing the day's
activities with a colleague.

7.50 am In the Dormy Clubhouse, which is the golfers' clubhouse and restaurant, Heather Edment is busy in the golf office. In fact, she is busy all day. There is someone starting on the first tee on all three golf courses every ten minutes and Heather is the lady the golfers come to when they want to book their tee times. She also deals with the administration, of which there is a considerable amount.

8.00 am Andy Hamer, the Premier Sous Chef or, in other words, the most important man in the kitchen after Executive Head Chef Mike Picken, arrives for the early shift. Norman Brockie has long since waved goodbye to his peace and quiet and the kitchen is now full of chefs and underchefs preparing for the beginning of another important and hectic day. Andy checks everything is running smoothly before holding a meeting with his staff in the staff canteen. They go over all the day's functions and banquets and Andy ensures everyone knows what they are doing. There are daily menu requests and Andy has to write out menus for future events. He discusses and follows up any complaints, checks the VIP guest list, and makes sure the numbers of people and the menus are correct. Then it's back to the kitchen, where he writes out the board for the restaurant staff to follow for the evening service. Andy also looks at what was ordered the previous day from the suppliers and checks the previous day's food cost to see if he is under or over budget.

8.00 am Porter Willie Jarvie arrives, ready to assist guests who are checking in and out. You need to be pretty fit to be a porter. 'Usually there are about 250 guests checking in and out of rooms each day. Each room has an average of five cases – so we can have over 1,000 cases going in and out. The lift's in the centre of the hotel and, given that it's about a quarter of a mile from one end of a wing to the other, the furthest wing is an eighth of a mile from the lift. It's not unusual for us porters to walk more than 20 miles in a day. It certainly keeps you fit!' explains Willie.

8.15 am Gordon Mair, the Systems Manager, arrives for work. The first thing he does is check that the computer system is working properly. Fidelio, as the system is called, is key to the smooth running of the hotel. Press a button and you can see at a glance how many rooms are full, what future reservations have been made, billing information, guest history etc. If Fidelio decides to go on strike there is a backup system, but problems at peak times can cause extreme disruption.

WILLIE JARVIE

8.30 am The suppliers deliver fresh food for the kitchen. Everything is checked and double-checked. Andy Hamer only accepts food that is in optimum condition. If an avocado looks slightly bruised then it is sent back. Sources are continually checked and re-checked. The hotel staff try to think of their suppliers as partners, with mutual trust and expectations. Andy Hamer gives an example of the high quality they expect: 'We have started using a brand of beef called Orkney Gold. Only 20 per cent of the beef coming out of the Orkneys gets the gold brand and only certain butchers are allowed to sell it. It is the best and the best is what we are looking for.'

The Glorious 12th signals the start of the grouse season and, five days later, guests are feasting on the Gleneagles grouse. Nothing is left to chance – unlike many restaurant staff, Andy knows the exact history of his grouse. 'I know that a dog called Zebedee picked the grouse (dead) off the ground at Braemar. It was then brought to our local butcher, Simon Howie of Auchterarder, who plucked and gutted it. It spent three days hanging in the butcher's shop and then was sent to us. We sell it within two days.' The same kind of attention to detail is applied to the fresh salmon which comes out of the River Tay, and indeed to all the food that is served at The Gleneagles Hotel.

8.30 am General Manager George Graham is holding his first meeting of the day. Known as 'morning prayers', it is a staff meeting to check the agenda for the day, such as which VIPs are expected; the non-resident functions; and also to review the previous day's work and agree changes and responsibilities for future events. George's role sits in perfect harmony with that of Managing Director Peter Lederer. 'I'm the captain steering the ship,' says George, 'and Peter's the MD of the shipping company deciding whether we should build a brand new ship or undertake a major makeover of the present one.' Some general managers retain a distance from the staff, but George Graham does whatever is necessary to ensure

21

SIMON HOWIE, *who provides the meat for the hotel, at work in his shop in the local village of Auchterarder.*

SENIOR
MANAGEMENT
*Managing Director Peter
Lederer (left) and General
Manager George Graham
discuss strategy at one of
their regular meetings.*

DEBBIE KNIGHT

the guests are well cared for. On a busy Saturday night, George might well be found parking cars or seating guests in The Strathearn, to help relieve the pressure on his staff.

9.00 am Having spent some time with her own bird, a Ferruginoos buzzard named Reg, Falconry School Manager Debbie Knight greets her first guests of the day. The young falcons are out with their keepers, being trained. Rather like learner pilots, they have to learn how to fly, hunt and (especially in Scotland) get used to the wind and rain. At six or seven weeks the birds are fully grown but need to build up fitness before flying in the display team. The falcons capture other birds in flight and are therefore spectacular creatures to hunt with. Dressed in Barbours and sturdy shoes and with their left hand cloaked in a special leather glove, today's falconers are ready for action.

As the falconers wait in eager anticipation, two Harris' Hawks are brought out. The Harris' Hawks are the labradors of the bird world, with an easy-going temperament and an outstanding hunting ability. Today French and her sister Saunders are going out hunting. Saunders is very instinctive and she and her sister are amongst the best hunting birds at The British School of Falconry. Short, sharp sprinters, the girls are ready to give the local rabbits a run for their money. The real sprinter among birds, the Goshawk, is a fast mover, but is prone to moods and is particularly difficult to maintain. Today Mr Goshawk will not be going out hunting as the hunters lack the necessary experience to cope with his fast, but temperamental character.

9.15 am The off road driving enthusiasts are arriving for a half day's 'Discover Scotland' scenic tour. They will drive down 1 in 3 gradients, through torrential rain and experience all the thrills and frights of the funfair, while learning a new and demanding skill.

9.30 am Action at The Jackie Stewart Shooting School. The clay pigeon enthusiasts begin their day under the direction of Shooting School Manager Chris Jenkins.

Set up by champion shot Jackie Stewart, the shooting school is the world's busiest clay target shooting school, and is open every day except Christmas Day. The school is popular with all the guests, including the Royal Family and the many business delegates and conference attendees who use the principles involved in shooting to guide them when they are developing valuable team-building exercises.

10.00 am The function rooms are being set up for buffets. A theme is usually chosen, for example, the 'Round Europe' buffet, which consists of four or five sections offering food from Scotland, France, Germany and Italy. The hotel staff try to add a bit of theatre to the proceedings. For the McDonalds' Women's PGA Championship of Europe they had a pizza oven to make fresh pizza, with staff making pasta and cooking *moules marinières* at the tables.

10.00 am The aquafit class is underway in The Club swimming pool. These classes are frequented mainly by ladies, although a few brave chaps do join in.

10.30 am A bread-making class begins for the children, led by one of the pastry chefs. It's fun, messy and great for entertaining the kids while mum and dad relax or take in a round of golf.

11.00 am Head Golf Professional Greg Schofield is heavily involved in golf instruction. 'I spend about a third to half my time teaching at The Golf Academy or playing golf,' he explains. 'The rest of the day is spent on administration and promoting and selling Gleneagles Golf. We also prepare packages or proposals for groups who might want a corporate day at Gleneagles, or something special for their staff or clients.' Greg sees a great deal of the club members. They form the core of his business and he helps them plan and organise their own tournaments. Naturally, Greg is also on hand to help them improve their game and to encourage each player to realise his or her potential.

11.30 am The lunch time buffet is ready. Andy Hamer is chief taster.

12.00 midday The Club restaurant is open for lunch. The early-morning golfers are in the Dormy Bar ordering ploughman's salads, cheese and bacon burgers, haggis, neeps 'n' tatties, lamb's liver and bacon and chipolatas, as they chat about the great rounds they nearly played, or will have played by the end of the afternoon!

12.00 midday – 1.00 pm This is peak time for the porters as the volume of guests checking in and out reaches its height. For porter Willie Jarvie it's all go, with guests arriving and leaving and other guests requesting transport around the resort to get to their various activities. The porters book restaurants and air tickets, organise transport to airports and railway stations and even walk dogs. They offer a truly personal service, not only walking Fido, so enabling the guest to sleep in or participate in a favourite sporting activity, but also running errands such as popping down to the local pharmacist

THE FUNCTION ROOMS

*G*LENEAGLES has ten function rooms which can be adapted to suit a range of events, from exhibitions and hospitality to grand dinner dances. The prestigious Gleneagles Suite is the best-equipped facility of its kind in the UK and can hold up to 400 people. Within the hotel are several first-class venues:

THE BALLROOM
holds up to 360 in a meeting, 400 for cocktails and 200 for dinner

GLENDEVON
holds up to 140 in a meeting, 200 for cocktails and 120 for dinner

BARONY
holds up to 100 in a meeting, 120 for cocktails and 70 for dinner

BRAIDS
holds up to 30 in a meeting, 80 for cocktails and 60 for dinner

RUTHVEN
holds up to 26 in a meeting, 70 for cocktails and 40 for dinner

TERRACE
holds up to 40 in a meeting, 70 for cocktails and 40 for dinner

ORCHIL
holds up to 30 in a meeting, 50 for cocktails and 30 for dinner

Conference facilities can also be provided outside the hotel itself in the Dormy Suite, which holds up to 60, and in the Grampian Suite, which holds up to 100.

23

in Auchterarder to pick up prescriptions. Perhaps the most unusual request came when a porter was asked to get a fax to a guest's friend who happened to be travelling on the Orient Express. The train cannot accept faxes, so it was a case of working out where the train was going to stop next and sending the fax there. The porters at Gleneagles remembered that the owners of the Orient Express also owned Turnberry Hotel and Golf Course. A call was made to the hotel and the train timetable obtained. At that moment the train was on its way from Paris to Istanbul. The Turnberry staff were able to say exactly where the train was and the fax arrived and was received successfully at the next station. Gleneagles had another satisfied customer.

3.00 pm Andy places the food orders for the next day with his suppliers.

3.00 pm Peter Lederer is back from his trip to London and in the boardroom to discuss strategy with his management team. Each member of the team is assigned a particular area of research – they have four days in which to study the issues and report back to Peter.

5.30 pm Peak rush hour in The Club as members and hotel guests hurry back from work, meetings or a day's gluttony in the hotel restaurants. The pool, gym, sauna and steam room are all in action.

7.30 pm Pre-dinner drinks in The Bar. Barman Magnus advises on cocktails and oversees what he describes as 'the most elegant drinks service in the world'. People are about to go into dinner and the atmosphere in The Bar has changed to one of anticipation of the delights to come.

Head Waiter Angus Macmillan is also busy in The Bar, taking wine orders and chatting to the guests. Angus uses all his experience of wine waiting to judge what a particular guest might order. The smartly dressed set tend to drink champagne, the tweed jacket set stick to classic wines and traditional aperitifs like malt whisky, and the younger, trendy set like to get to know the New World wines.

Some guests have most discerning tastes. One Swiss gentleman is particularly partial to a Lafitte 1923 – a mere snip at £900 a bottle. If you really want to push the boat out you can go for a bottle of Petrus 1970. It will set you back £1,700. Your bank account may be empty but the exquisite taste will remain with you long after you've left the hotel.

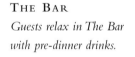

THE BAR

Guests relax in The Bar with pre-dinner drinks.

8.00 pm Peter Lederer is hosting a dinner for guests who are all involved in the tourist industry. First up is a lively discussion on the economy and devolution, and then it's on to the main course. As usual, the Gleneagles restaurant staff, with their ever-present smiles and their unfailing good humour, provide a first-class service.

9.00 pm Restaurant Manager Elaine Watson and her colleagues are experiencing peak rush hour in the dining room. The kitchens are also under great pressure. The conferences, banquets and buffets are all being served with their specially selected menus, but the dining room requirements are not finalised until the last moment. The waiters and waitresses are taught to skillfully encourage guests to select the various delicacies on offer, but, inevitably, some guests will want favourites that are not on the menu. Mike Picken and his team always try to satisfy the demand for special requests. A happy guest means a happy hotel, and this is never more true than in the kitchens.

   This is the time when the guests who haven't decided where to eat, or the 'floating guests', as they are known, make up their minds and descend upon their chosen eating outlet. When the figure for floating guests hits 100 the kitchen and restaurant staff start to feel a little edgy. They will only relax when all the orders have been made and delivered to everyone's satisfaction.

THE STRATHEARN
RESTAURANT
The splendour of the main restaurant creates a dining experience to be savoured.

26

THE CHEFS

*A chef's life is often hectic.
In the kitchens everyone
plays their part to ensure
that the guests enjoy a
world-class dining
experience.*

10.00 pm Night Chef Carlton Doudney takes over the kitchen for the night. It's a tough life living in the twilight zone, working when everyone is sleeping and sleeping when everyone is working. Carlton still finds it punishing. 'It's fine when you are in the swing of it,' he explains, 'but after a couple of days off it's difficult to get going again. It's not so bad in winter, but motivation can be a problem when it's a beautiful sunny day outside and you've only had a few hours' sleep!'

Carlton is in charge of room service and bar orders. He also helps with the following morning's breakfasts by preparing the cold buffet, making up the large fruit bowls and laying out the cold meats and smoked salmon on trays. Then he prepares the hot stuff, ready for Norman to cook when he arrives in the small hours. He lays out the sausages and bacon and makes up the scrambled egg in the pan, ready to be cooked.

Breakfast can be for 50 or 500, and if its nearer the latter then Norman will need all the preparation help he can get. If the guests have been fishing they'll bring back the trout and ask for it to be cooked for breakfast.

It is difficult to accurately plan for room service. There can be 1, 10 or 100 orders. Each night is different. The most popular item is the Club Sandwich, followed closely by The Gleneagles Burger. Some people stray from the menu, but Carlton always tries his best to keep them happy. 'People request dishes that aren't on the menu. If I have the ingredients then I'll do it. Bacon sandwiches are a good example – they're not on the menu but we sell loads of them.' Carlton likes the fact that he is his own boss and can make these decisions without having to refer to anyone else.

10.15 pm The first *après*-dinner guests are filtering into The Bar for drinks. A group of malt whisky lovers appears and Magnus goes into action. Malt whisky is his speciality. Magnus has researched his cherished subject in depth and is now considered something of an expert. Speyside (between Aberdeen and Elgin) is the acknowledged heartland of whisky production and two of the guests are familiar with Mortlach and Glenlossie, so Magnus gives them a 16-year old Mortlach and a 15-year old Glenlossie, served in small brandy balloons, which are the ideal glasses from which to 'nose' and taste the malts. Both men are satisfied. The Mortlach is a rich, smooth malt with a sweetish, nutty, dry finish, and the Glenlossie has a delightful odour of green apples and pear drops. The other guest decides to be a little more adventurous and go for a malt that is more complex, which he hasn't tried before. Magnus thinks for a moment and then produces a rare malt, a 23-year old Glenury Royal. A stunning rich gold in colour, the Glenury Royal has a complex flavour – a trace of sherry reflecting the original use of its cask, and overtones of peat smoke. Everyone is satisfied. Like The Gleneagles Hotel, Scottish malt whisky is steeped in mysticism and folklore. It defies analysis and retains the secrets that make it impossible to reproduce in any other country.

MALT TASTING
Barman Magnus Heron organises an impromptu tasting for a couple of whisky devotees.

28

A LITTLE LUXURY
For those guests who desire
a little more space, the
hotel also offers a number
of sumptuously decorated
luxury suites.

10.40 pm Max has a 20-minute handover period before he has to take his turn as duty manager.

11.00 pm Max takes over the night shift. Like Carlton, he has never quite got used to working in the twilight zone. 'By March I feel desperate for some sunshine,' he says. 'I look like a milk bottle!' There are seven night auditors in doing the books, preparing bills and financial reports. The first thing Max does is conduct a tour of the whole resort to gauge the atmosphere and pick up on any potential problems. Usually it's all running smoothly. He checks the Gents and asks a female member of staff to check the Ladies – things do have a tendency to go walkabouts. As he says, 'Sometimes pictures sprout legs and move. Usually they get five yards and are discovered behind a sofa or under a table in the bar.'

11.30 pm Max makes sure all the finances are in order. He checks that the room rates and billing instructions are all correct.

12.10 am Peter Lederer has not turned into a pumpkin and is on his way home. It's almost 19 hours since he left home for the airport.

12.30 am First major problem for Max. A horse has escaped from The Equestrian Centre. There's a blizzard outside and the horse is white. 'It was a nightmare,' he says. 'It took twenty minutes to locate the animal. I think I'd driven past him halfway along the road to Crieff. In the end the police found him and we enticed him into the horsebox with sweets.'

1.30 am Two guests, a girl and her fiancé, arrive in the kitchen to keep Carlton company. They run a pub/restaurant and are eager to find out how the Gleneagles kitchen operates. They are so impressed they stay for two hours.

1.45 am Another visitor in the kitchen for Carlton. Who ever said night-time was the quiet time? Carlton's visitor is clearly under the influence, holding up well, but showing signs of a 'drink effect'. Someone has bet him he can't find a trolley and push one of his friends down the hotel corridor on it. 'Given that there were loads of empty trolleys behind me,' says Carlton, 'I could hardly get away with saying that we didn't have any. Fortunately, his sober wife came to my rescue and carefully led him away!'

2.00 am The computer begins the night audit.

2.15 am The night porters start to collect the luggage from outside the rooms of those guests who will be leaving early in the morning.

3.00 am Carlton cooks for the night staff. Pasta, pizza or steak and chips plus dessert – the staff are treated to three courses. Carlton is just finishing off this preparation when two guests decide they fancy something 'Chinesy'. Carlton obliges and produces a chicken stir-fry. They are so impressed they come down to the kitchen to thank him personally.

3.15 am Max is going over the banqueting details for the next day and checking with room service that the right shoes are outside the right room. It isn't unusual for shoes to wander in the middle of the night and end up outside someone else's door. As he is checking each floor he finds a man asleep outside the door of his room. He couldn't get the room card to work so decided to sleep where he was rather than walk back to the lifts and go down to Reception. Max lets him in so he can sleep in more comfort.

3.30 am Carlton is having a coffee break and Norman arrives for the start of a new day.

29

ROOM FOR ALL
THE FAMILY
*Gleneagles' youngest guest
finds time for a quick
afternoon nap.*

CHAPTER TWO

The Early Years

Wit and Grace and Love and Beauty
In ae constellation shine!
To adore thee is my duty,
Goddess o' this soul o' mine!

FROM 'BONNIE WEE THING'
ROBERT BURNS

ONALD MATHESON was the man who turned the dream of The Gleneagles Hotel into a stunning reality. He had a vision of a highland palace, that would sit in the splendour of the hills and glens of the Strathearn valley. From this vision came the hotel that would entrance the world.

It all started in 1910 when Donald Matheson, newly promoted to the position of General Manager of The Caledonian Railway Company, spent a holiday in the Strathearn region and was captivated by the sheer beauty of his surroundings. When the holiday was over he returned to work determined to convince his fellow directors of the advantages of building a magnificent hotel in the Highlands. They readily agreed and the plans began.

Donald Matheson had died by the time his great grandson Nigel Kenyon was born, but his strength of character and forceful personality remain legendary within the family and Mr Kenyon remembers family tales of the old man's business philosophy. 'In Grandfather Matheson's day,' Nigel explains, 'the railways ruled supreme as the most used form of transport. This was the era of great expansion in rail travel, before planes and cars took a hold as a means of transport. Grandfather Matheson bought or built hotels in the city as he saw this as a natural extension of his railway business. Given that golf was already a major pastime, it made sense to marry a magnificent sport with a magnificent hotel.'

The landowners of the site chosen for Gleneagles were a family called the Denby Roberts, and the land remains in their hands today. Unlike the Dukes of Westminster and other notable English families, however, the Denby Roberts have not made their fortune out of The Gleneagles Hotel. The land is known as 'fe' land, which is short for feudal, meaning that only a nominal rent is paid. Today, Sir William Denby Roberts is a benevolent neighbour. A member of The Club, he believes that The Gleneagles Hotel has

OPPOSITE:
EARLY VISITORS
The Gleneagles Hotel,
with its magnificent
Highland setting, soon
became a home from home
for the leisured classes of
the early 1900s.

30

brought valuable employment to the area and is good news for local people. His father, however, took a rather different view of things: 'Dad thought that Gleneagles was a den of iniquity, as there were lots of "goings on" between people who weren't married. He would get extremely irritated whenever he heard about some high society capers, or the Maharajah of somewhere or other arriving with several wives in tow!'

In 1913, after a couple of years of planning and discussion, a company known as Gleneagles Ltd was formed. The company was charged with constructing and operating the hotel, and planning the golf courses. The Caledonian Railway Company agreed to contribute up to £25,000 in building finance, and a service railway was built between the nearby station at Auchterarder and the hotel site for the transportation of materials (this was also used to transport guests and luggage to the hotel's back door).

In 1914, the outbreak of the First World War brought proceedings to an undignified halt and the hotel remained a roofless shell for the next nine years. Many people doubted whether it would ever be completed but they had clearly underestimated the determination and tenacity of Donald Matheson.

A GRAND OPENING

At the opening night gala of Saturday the 7th of June 1924, Donald Matheson finally witnessed the splendid realisation of his dream. The press were unanimous in their praise, calling the new hotel 'The Playground of the Gods', 'The Switzerland of Scotland', and 'The Highland Palace'.

Even without its impressive structure and facilities Gleneagles would have made the headlines, as the music at the opening ball was broadcast all over Britain by the BBC. In the 1920s this was something of a technical miracle. The sound was amplified, put over a land line to Glasgow, and transmitted from there. Some of the guests went up to their rooms and listened to the music that was being played live downstairs coming out of their wirelesses!

The band leader, Henry Hall, went on to achieve considerable fame and his signature tune, 'Come ye back to Bonnie Scotland', was heard all over the country. Henry Hall wrote a piece of music especially for the opening night called 'Glen of Eagles'. It was a medley of four tunes. The first was dedicated to James Braid, five-times winner of the British Open Golf Championship and designer of two of the Gleneagles golf courses, the second tune honoured Gordon Lockhart, the first Gleneagles golf professional, the third praised Arthur Towle, the Controller of London, Midland and Scottish Railways (which had absorbed The Caledonian Railway Company) and the fourth was an ode to the village of Auchterarder.

The motto of The Gleneagles Hotel was 'Heich abune the Heich' (High above the High), reflecting the hotel's mission to provide a service that stood head and shoulders above the rest.

TRAVELLING WITH THE ROYALS

Mr Matheson was a truly extraordinary man, living a lifestyle that has long since faded into distant memory. Nigel Kenyon recalls the manner in which Donald Matheson and his wife Agnes travelled when King George V and Queen Mary were due at Balmoral. 'Grandfather and grandma had a suite in the Central Hotel in Glasgow. When they wished to travel, the stationmaster would escort them to

RAIL LINK
The station in 1923, one year before the grand opening of the hotel.

33

ROYAL
CONNECTIONS
*King George V and
Queen Mary, seen here
with Prince Edward VIII,
were friends of Donald
Matheson and special
guests of the hotel.*

the platform, where they would board their own train, which consisted of two engines and two carriages, the general manager's day carriage and his night carriage. They would then travel down to London in splendour.

'Once in London, the royal train, which consisted of about five carriages, would be hitched up in the middle of Grandfather Matheson's train, and then they would all set off for the Highlands. Somewhere around Watford, the King's equerry would appear in grandfather's carriage and say something along the lines of, "Their Majesties request the pleasure of the company of Mr and Mrs Matheson for dinner." And so grandpa and granny would get dressed and toddle down to the royal dining car.'

It was a great honour to be invited to dine with King George V and Queen Mary, as the Royals were not by nature sociable people. The King was somewhat reticent in his manner and Queen Mary was a rather guttural German. They tended to dine on a table just about big enough for a game of cards – hardly the sign of people who loved socialising.

It was an enduring friendship, however, and when Grandpa Matheson died in 1935, aged 75, and having been awarded the MVO (Member of the Victorian Order), the King and Queen sent a telegram to his widow. It read, 'The King and Queen much regret to hear of the death of Mr Donald Matheson, of whom they preserve many pleasant recollections. Their Majesties assure you and your family of their true sympathy in your bereavement.'

THE MATHESON FAMILY

The bond between Mr Matheson and the King and Queen came from a meeting of minds. Donald Matheson was a very charming and kind man, but he found it

HAROLD WARDLE

*I*N THE 1920s and 1930s jobs were relatively scarce. Most working people took what they could and considered themselves lucky if they had a roof over their heads and food on the table. Harold Wardle reckoned a job as a waiter would mean he would never go hungry. He started his career as a commis waiter in the Adelphi Hotel in Liverpool, one of the hotels that belonged to London, Midland and Scottish Railways, before joining Gleneagles and working his way up to become Head Waiter.

Harold's father was a skilled cabinet-maker, but unfortunately had been laid off during the Great Depression. One of the advantages of Harold's job at the Adelphi was that he could save some food from the hotel meals to give to his father and mother.

A spell in Paris, working at the 1918 Peace Conference and learning French, was followed by a period in Madrid, where Harold learnt Spanish. In 1924 he was sent to Gleneagles to work as Second Head Waiter.

Romance blossomed for Harold one day when he spied a young waitress in the corridor and decided immediately this was the girl he was going to marry. Harold and Elsie married in 1927. They lived an idyllic existence. The position of Head Waiter had a lot of influence in those days – Harold could hire and fire, and the waiters obeyed his every command. The guests were very demanding and used to living a cocooned existence, and so it was imperative that the dining room ran like clockwork.

In 1930 Harold said goodbye to Gleneagles and joined the Caledonian Hotel in Edinburgh. Some years later, Harold the father took Harold the son to Gleneagles to watch a football match between the combined team of the North British and Caledonian Hotels in Edinburgh and a team of waiters from Gleneagles. The Italian and French waiters of Gleneagles had the talent, and put on the style. By half-time the score was 20-0, so father and son capitulated and retired to the staff dining room.

For son Harold this was paradise, especially when the head waiter produced a hand-made *millefeuille* gateau. 'It was six inches high, with layer upon layer of wafer-thin pastry, filled with cream and jam,' says Harold. 'When I was allowed to take the remains of the gateau home I truly felt I had died and gone to heaven!'

The Gleneagles waiters line up in 1926, with Harold Wardle 6th from left on the second row. The head waiters are distinguished by their black bow ties.

35

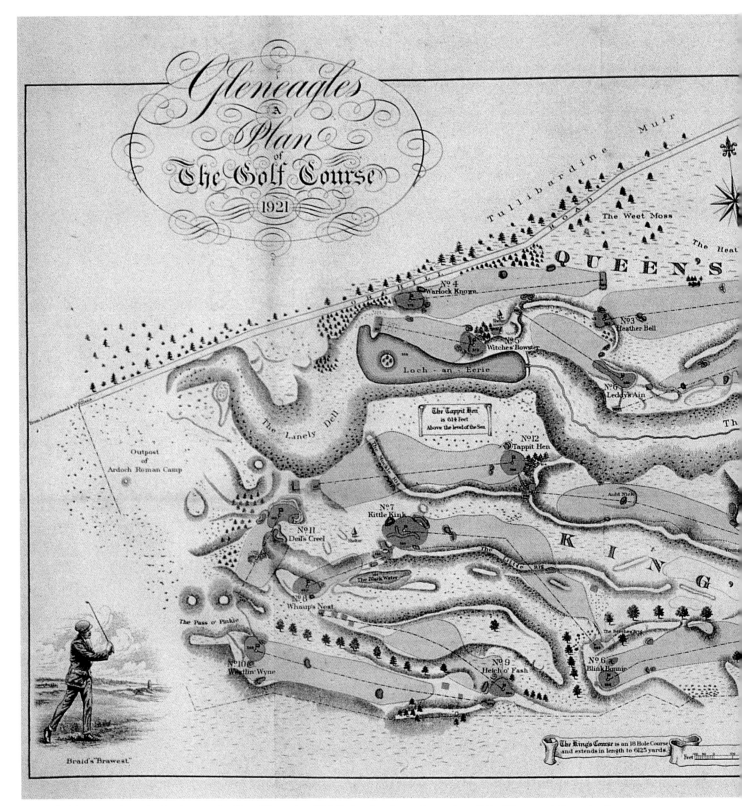

BRAID'S DESIGN *An early sketch map of golf at Gleneagles (1921) showing the perfect setting of The King's and Queen's Courses.*

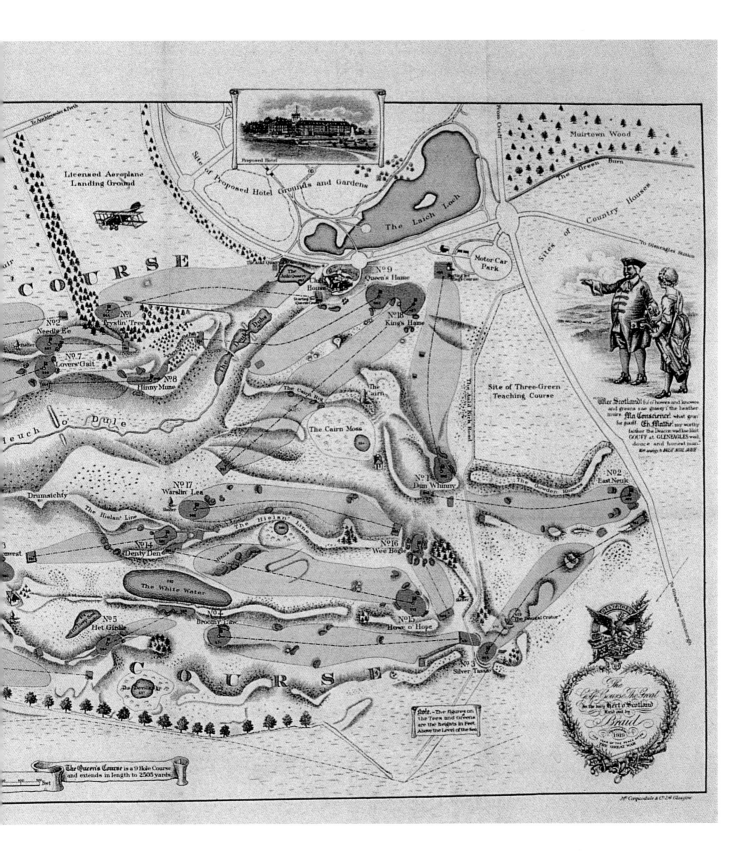

JIM LAWSON – CONQUERING KING'S

ONE MAN who remembers the formality of the early years as well as the fun is Jim Lawson. Mr Lawson, now in his 90th year, is still as bright-eyed and alert as he was when, as a 16-year-old golfer, he won the Furniture Trades Open Competition on the famed King's Course, and was treated to dinner in the 'big house' afterwards.

Born on the 8th of November 1910, in Biggar, Lanarkshire, Mr Lawson has enjoyed a lasting love affair with golf. By the age of 16 he was already playing off a handicap of 8, and his success astounded the Resident Golf Professional, Gordon Lockhart,

who remarked, 'If you hadn't had a professional caddy with you, your card of 47 points would have been viewed with suspicion.'

Jim Lawson's stunning round on The King's Course would remain etched in everyone's memory. Eighty years on Jim can still remember every detail of the day he became the Tiger Woods of the early 1900s. 'The 18th hole on The King's is the most difficult as it changes contour about 3 times,' says Jim. 'It's very important to get the drive in the right section of the fairway. You have to get your 2nd shot in the right place to get a good entry

on the 3rd shot. I scored 6 points on 3 successive holes by holing a shot 180 yards for a net 2 on a par 5, at which I had 1 stroke. The next hole was a par 4 and I holed it in 3. Two holes after the short hole, I had a hole in one, which was my 2nd hole in one of the round. I picked up 7 shots in 3 holes.'

Three years after his dazzling round on The King's, Jim Lawson met Gordon Lockhart again. Lockhart was always immaculately dressed in plus fours with a matching flat cap in black and white checked tweed. Jim Lawson had volunteered to act as caddy for one of four golf professionals who were competing in a tournament. By chance, his name was drawn with that of Gordon Lockhart. After playing a few holes, Mr Lockhart turned to the young Mr Lawson and said, 'I think I've met you before. Have you ever been to Gleneagles?' Jim Lawson replied, 'I was there once and I put in a score which you viewed with grave suspicion, before accepting the word of the professional caddy.' They both laughed at the memory and carried on with the game.

The golf and the society style that accompanied it soon put Gleneagles firmly on the map and made it an essential destination on any golf lover's pilgrimage. Americans soon discovered Gleneagles and made it an important part of their European tour.

Jim Lawson (left) and Mr Bird, his partner for the day, in 1974. That day Jim Lawson played a round that marked 50 years playing with a single figure handicap.

difficult to relate to people on an emotional level. When his son-in-law was lost in the First World War, he took on paternal responsibility for his son-in-law's daughters and sent them to be educated at Cheltenham Ladies College. His letters to them were full of details of board meetings and business, rather than tales of pet rabbits or the sort of stories likely to amuse and interest young girls. One thing the contents did reveal, however, was the close friendship between Donald Matheson and Sir Robert McAlpine. In one letter, he wrote, 'Stuart [Matheson's son] and Alfred and Robert Junior [Sir Robert McAlpine's sons] are getting on so well that we might consider putting a company together.' Unfortunately, fate intervened and the young Stuart died from an incurable disease in 1927, aged 26. This not only broke Donald Matheson's heart, and turned him into a bit of a recluse, but also prevented the Matheson son being linked to the McAlpine family, whose name would become famous as their construction company expanded to become a major international conglomerate.

Granny Matheson, Donald's wife, enjoyed the luxurious lifestyle, but, like many ladies in the early 1900s, was naïve when it came to the ways of the world. When Gleneagles first opened she would often sit outside the front door waving to people and treating the hotel as her own personal home. She thought it belonged to her husband, as it had been his idea to build it!

Auntie Fluff, one of Matheson's two daughters, never married and died in 1989, aged 89. But the female line continued through her sister, Agnes, whose daughter married Nigel Kenyon's father Derek in 1939. Derek Kenyon had the same energy and commitment to the pursuit of excellence as Donald Matheson,

A SPECTATOR SPORT

The popularity of golf increased during the 1930s and attracted a devoted following. Spectators flocked to The King's Course to watch the tournaments of the era.

A GRAND HOTEL
The path to comfort and luxury.

which were qualities that the Matheson women admired in their men. On the morning of his wedding Mr Kenyon played a round of golf at Royal Troon and on the 8th hole, which is 126 yards long and one of the most famous short holes in the world of golf (the green is so tiny that it is known as 'The Postage Stamp'), he achieved a hole in one. Then he went off and got married.

The happy couple decided to spend their honeymoon at Gleneagles. When they arrived at the hotel, the porter was reading a copy of the evening newspaper which had a photograph of the wedding on the front page. The secret was out. The next day on the golf course, when Derek Kenyon took his first golf club out of the bag, he and his companions were covered in confetti! No-one was left in any doubt as to his status as a newly wed husband.

A CHARMED LIFE

With the hotel's reputation growing by the day, it wasn't long before the rich and famous started to spend the summer season at Gleneagles. In the 1920s, London society spent its summer outside the City – as the Court left Buckingham Palace, the aristocrats tended to follow.

Class distinction was considered the natural order in the 1920s and 1930s and the privileged classes enjoyed a lifestyle seemingly untouched by the Great Depression of the 1930s. This did not really change until the Second World War altered people's lives completely. Meanwhile, there was a lot of partying to be done. Sir William Denby Roberts remembers tales of such vigorous dancing of reels in the ballroom that the mirrors would tremble and fall off the walls.

In the summer season the suites tended to be occupied by the same person for at least three to four weeks. Each guest would throw a cocktail party for the other occupants of the suites. There was a definite rhythm to life. There was no such thing as 24-hour room service and eating in the dining room at 11.00 pm was unheard of. You ate and relaxed at the appointed times. And people always dressed for dinner. The diners would dazzle in their finery and the dining room service was expected to match.

The 216 bedrooms offered accommodation for 350 guests. The garage could accommodate 80 cars and the dining room could seat 300 guests, while 200 couples filled the ballroom to dance to Henry Hall's band. During the summer season the hotel was full, not only with British aristocrats and rich industrialists, but also with distinguished foreign guests.

We may think we have become blasé about travel – today London, tonight New York, tomorrow Sydney – but the rich Americans of the 1920s were hardly different in their attitude to travel. As Mr Kenyon recalls, they would arrive in England on the great old liners, and simply drive their cars off the ship as though they were still in Manhattan. 'A lot of the American guests would live in grand townhouses on 5th Avenue,' he explains, 'and when they came to England for "the season", they would simply pack up the house, put it in the car, or cars, along with their servants, and transport everything on the grand old ships. They were

HOTEL PARTY
During the 1930s, wealthy families and their friends would flock to The Gleneagles Hotel to spend the summer season.

41

BESSIE ROBINSON – UPSTAIRS DOWNSTAIRS

essie Robinson arrived at Gleneagles as an assistant chambermaid in 1926. Her father was a seafaring man, who drowned when she was young, so she had a hard start in life.

At Gleneagles her day started at 5.30 am, when a porter would knock on the door of the bedroom she shared with seven other girls. They were expected to get up, wash, put on their dark blue uniforms and be ready to start work by 6.00 am.

Bessie, her lifelong friend Lilian, and their colleagues began by cleaning and dusting the front hall and all the public rooms. Then it was upstairs to the second floor, which included the Royal Lochnagar Suite, 25 bedrooms and 8 suites.

One chambermaid and one assistant cleaned all the rooms. There were no vacuum cleaners – the carpets were cleaned with a bristle (which had a very hard, long shaft) and sweeper.

At 8.00 am a breakfast of porridge was served and at 8.30 am it was back to work until 3.00 pm, with just one half-hour break for lunch. Between 3.00 and 5.00 pm the girls were off duty. Bessie's mother lived in nearby Auchterarder and would push Bessie's younger brother up the hill in his pram to visit her daughter during the two-hour break. They would bring Bessie some food to cheer her up and give her strength – usually a small milk flagon and some mince and 'tatties.

Between 5.00 and 9.00 pm Bessie and Lilian were on duty to clean

Right to left: Bessie Robinson, Sheila Perera and Lilian Hoult.

rooms or provide fresh linen and towels. At 9.00 pm the commis waiters would come into the staff restaurant with the leftovers from the dining room for the chambermaids.

The below stairs workers put in an average 78-hour week with one half-day off. Bessie earned the grand sum of 11 shillings a week (55p in today's money). At weekends, in addition to their cleaning jobs, the girls would be expected to take turns on duty in the ladies' cloakroom until 1.00 or 2.00 am, while the guests danced the night away in the ballroom.

On the plus side, the staff were never too cold, as the central heating pipes were located just outside their quarters. In the days when conditions in some hotels were so appalling that staff could literally freeze, this was a bonus not to be scoffed at.

In spite of the huge differences between life above and below stairs, Bessie retains an affection for her

former workplace. 'We had a fearsome housekeeper, a strict Aberdonian named Miss Williamson. She would inspect our uniforms every day, but was also nice and kind and would allow us to eat the dining room leftovers. I had never seen anything like Gleneagles. The hotel was very grand. No-one was allowed through the front door without a collar and tie and the guests would arrive in style. Most of the ladies brought their maids with them and they always dressed very formally for dinner. The beautiful dresses and jewels would fill the dining room, the lounge and the ballroom.'

In 1990, Gleneagles invited Bessie and Lilian to a VIP return to the hotel, to thank them for their years of toil.

'We travelled by first-class train,' says Bessie, 'and stayed in the Royal Lochnagar Suite. It was marvellous.'

incredibly laid-back about travelling halfway around the world for a few weeks' holiday. They thought of the travel simply as a nice journey, and as a prelude to a whole load of partying. I think that nowadays we have lost that ability to really enjoy ourselves and relax for extended periods. Now it's all about quick breaks and packing as many activities as possible in for a day or two before moving on.'

In 1926 Mr and Mrs Alan Butler literally did pop in. They flew their privately owned aircraft from Suffolk to Gleneagles in only three hours and forty minutes. At Gleneagles, the novelty and the challenge of air travel provided an excuse for an air rally, organised over the weekend of the 13th of May 1929. Captain W R Bailey and Mr W L Box arrived with their golf clubs strapped on to the side of the aircraft, while Miss Murielle Classen – at only 14, the youngest member of the Scottish Flying Club – and Mr R E Adams and his passenger, Miss W S Brown, arrived with suitcases ready for a weekend of fun. In an aircraft that was more suited to First World War flying aces, it was clear that the guests relished a challenge.

43

TEEING OFF
A couple tee-off in sight of the starter's hut on The King's Course in the 1930s.

The hotel did its best to protect its high-flying, high society guests from the press when they requested privacy, but the society columns of the main newspapers and magazines such as *Tatler* were frequently running pictures of the well-bred and famous, such as 'Mr Lloyd George at Gleneagles playing golf' and printing photographs of other public figures.

Donald Matheson had set the tone for The Gleneagles Hotel when he first conceived it as a grand but friendly establishment which would combine luxury with a homely welcome. Today he would be proud to see that those same characteristics, which both ensured the hotel's survival through the horrors of the Second World War and helped it re-establish itself afterwards, are more in evidence than ever.

Gleneagles
Wondermazes

HOTEL
GOLF
TENNIS
"Nonesuch in Europe"

Gleneagles Hotel and Golf Courses

"The Eighth Wonder"   LMS

EUROPEAN HOTSPOT
The Gleneagles Hotel was recognised as one of the leading sporting destinations for travellers in Europe.

CHAPTER THREE

The War Years: *from* Hotel *to* Hospital

Ae fond kiss, and then we sever,–
Ae fareweel, and then – for ever
Deep in heart-wrung tears I'll pledge thee!
Warring sighs and groans I'll wage thee!

FROM 'AE FOND KISS'
ROBERT BURNS

44

N JULY 1939 JIM LAWSON, whom we encountered previously breaking records on The King's Course, was serving as Works and Contracts Director for Thomas Love & Sons, an auctioneer based in Perth. By that time, everyone had come to the realisation that war was inevitable. One day, Jim received a call from 'the big house', as Gleneagles was often referred to in the region.

Mr Lawson takes up the story: 'We were asked to quote for supplying blackout curtains for the whole of Gleneagles. The word from the hotel was that it was no use waiting for war to be declared. War was on the way and the blackout curtains were needed double-quick. Our quote was accepted. We had said it would take four weeks for the curtains to be ready. In fact, they were ready in just two.'

Thomas Shields of Perth, who was the world's leading manufacturer of printed damask table covers, supplied the curtains. Blackout curtains had to be made of extremely dense cloth (the cloth for the Gleneagles curtains had 1,076 threads per square inch) and damask was the perfect material to use for this.

The blackout curtains signalled the beginning of the hotel's preparations for the serious business of war. The era of partying, dining and socialising was over. For the next six years The Gleneagles Hotel would trade its ballgowns and finery for the uniforms of the medical staff, as it transformed itself into one of the world's leading military hospitals.

OPPOSITE:
ALL CHANGE
As war raged through Europe, nights of partying were put on hold, as the hotel took on the more serious role of providing a haven for the sick.

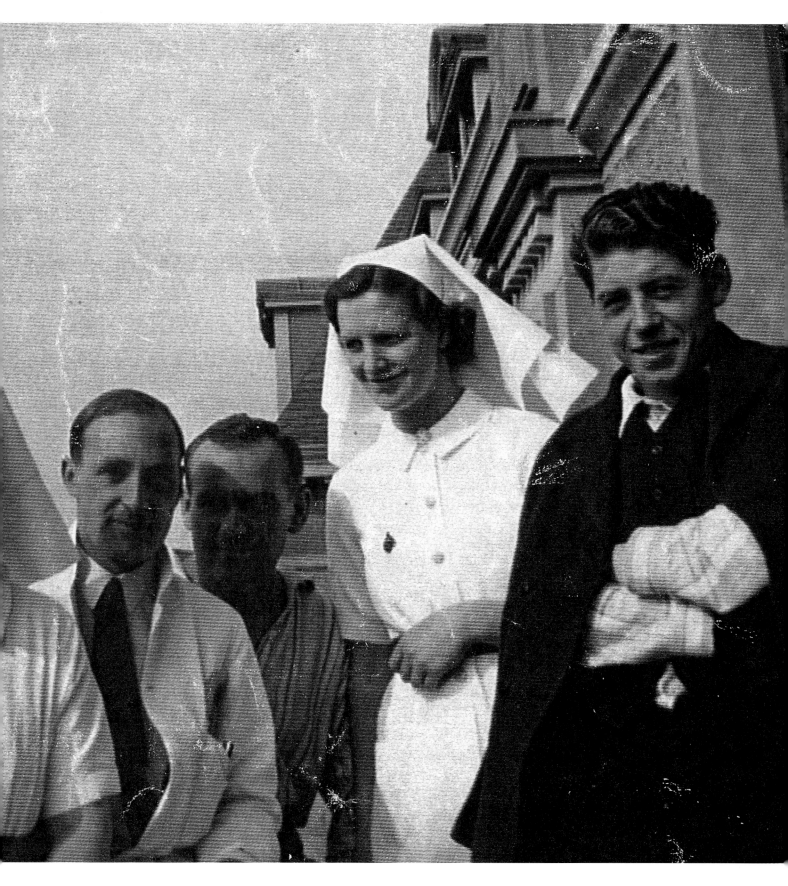

46

WELCOME VISITORS

Hundreds of sick and wounded were welcomed at the hotel-come-hospital. Above is one of the last groups of patients to be treated. They left in 1941.

A HAVEN FOR THE SICK

Mary Noble was a young woman who moved to the hotel, or hospital, as it had become, in March 1940, to take up the position of Senior Ward Sister. She was in charge of 63 patients, with 2 junior sisters to assist her. With Mary heavily involved in the war effort and her father working as a shipbuilder, this was the start of a very busy few years for the Noble family.

Before anyone had time to ponder on the complexities of war, the first casualties started to arrive at Gleneagles. The nurses had just a temporary uniform – Mary's red armband identified her as a senior sister. Despite the long hours and the often harrowing scenes she witnessed, Mary loved her job. The only thing she disliked was rising early in the morning. As she says, 'My family always said to me, "You're a grand riser at night, Mary," and I was.'

The standard of medical care at Gleneagles was exceptional, and had to be, as the casualties of an increasingly bloody war began to arrive needing care and attention. There were no antibiotics available, just the famous M&B (May and

FLORENCE MacMILLAN

THE SURGEONS did not only care for the servicemen, but tended to the local people as well. Florence MacMillan, who was ten years old in 1941, is an example of a civilian who owes her life to the skill of the Gleneagles surgeons.

Florence was an evacuee from the Clydebank blitz who was sent to Auchterarder, along with the rest of her classmates at Hillhead High School, during the war. In the autumn of 1941 she fell off her bicycle and badly injured her leg. She was taken to Gleneagles hospital and was fortunate to have some of the best surgeons in the world at hand when septicaemia set in.

Florence knows that if it hadn't been for the brilliance of the surgeons she might not have lived to tell the tale. 'When I arrived at the hospital, I wasn't too ill, but the wound became infected and so I needed urgent treatment. The hospital tried to get in touch with my parents, but they were not at home.

'As my life was at stake, the surgeon agreed to take complete responsibility for my treatment. The surgeon saved my life by opening up my leg and inserting rubber tubes to drain out the infection. Perhaps in another hospital I might not have survived, but in a military hospital like Gleneagles you could rest safe in the knowledge that the surgeons had specialist skills and were used to these complex operations.

'I was on my way to the operating theatre when my parents found a telegram from the hospital informing them of my condition. Of course they came straight away, and after that would come up on the train every weekend from Glasgow to see me. In those days there were no taxis, so my parents would walk up the drive from the station.'

Florence's friend, Alexa Walker, was another of her regular visitors. Before her accident, the two girls would play in the fields around Gleneagles and, during the winter that Florence spent in hospital, Alexa would skate alone on the frozen pond there. Florence couldn't help feeling a terrible pang of jealousy when she thought of her friend having fun skating on the ice without her.

Florence was admitted to Ward D (the female ward), which she shared with two Wrens. Ward D was in fact band leader Henry Hall's old room, and Florence remembers being very impressed with the large *en suite* bathroom, complete with sunken bath, which was very opulent for its day. 'We had to go down some steps to get into the sunken bath and I thought it was absolutely amazing. I'd never seen anything like it.'

Florence spent a total of 17 weeks in Ward D, and was there for the 1941 Christmas period.

Being the only child on the ward, Florence was spoilt rotten by the other patients, especially the Americans and Canadians, who were not subject to rationing and who therefore were not limited in the food and gifts they could offer.

Once she was feeling a little stronger, Florence would be wheeled along in a wicker bathchair to the ENSA (Entertainments National Service Association) concerts, which were held once or twice a week in the hotel, and the other patients would fill the foot of her wheelchair with sweets and chocolates.

Florence has particularly fond memories of Christmas Day: 'My surgeon, Mr Pollitt, gave me the book *Black Beauty* by Anna Sewell as a present, and we had a wonderful Christmas dinner. My parents presented me with a copy of 'A Nightingale Sang in Berkeley Square', which was a beautiful love song made popular by Vera Lynn. Every time I hear it I am immediately transported back to Gleneagles.

'I was very lucky to be so well looked after, and I was very aware of how badly injured some of the patients were. The Dunkirk boys were there – they would come along to the concerts and sit there wrapped up in bandages.'

Florence went on to train as a radiographer and work at the Glasgow Western Infirmary. She married an officer in the Royal Navy and they had three daughters.

She still retains fond and vivid memories of her time in hospital at Gleneagles and of the special atmosphere of the place during wartime. Her gratitude to the skilful surgeons remains undiminished, and in this she is no different from all the soldiers and local people treated there.

Baker) 125, an arsenic compound, and M&B 693, a well-known cure for bacterial pneumonia. Unsophisticated anaesthetics like ether were commonly used.

Life at Gleneagles during the war was dictated by the rhythm of the hospital trains – servicemen would arrive on the trains and have to be admitted as quickly as possible. In April 1940 the first hospital train brought servicemen injured in the battle of Narvik in Norway. Miss Noble remembers the departure and arrival of the train vividly. 'The hospital train was fully equipped and had its own staff. The Sister who worked on the train was ready to leave at a moment's notice, as were her staff. The train would go anywhere it was required. If more staff were needed then Sister would ring and ask for a qualified nurse. We would never refuse the request, as the trains were the first point of contact for injured servicemen and the treatment they received while travelling could be the difference between life and death. One night a convoy of Polish patients arrived at the back door. We admitted 100 patients in 20 minutes.'

Patients would be dressed in navy-blue trousers and white shirts, with a waterproof band around their wrist. In this would be an envelope stating which drugs they had to take and what their injuries were. The nurses would check the envelopes to see whether the men needed to be admitted to a surgical or a medical ward. All the wards were identified by letters rather than numbers and the patients would have the number of the ward they were assigned to chalked on their forehead, so that their correct destination could be quickly identified.

Speed and efficiency were of the essence, not only to save lives but also to avoid detection by the enemy. Even the golf course bunkers were filled in to avoid detection. Yet in the rush to admit everyone, the staff never missed an opportunity to make the lives of the injured more comfortable.

As Miss Noble recalls, 'We had two Polish patients, one who spoke good English and one who didn't, so we woke up a couple of Scottish boys who were in for treatment and asked them if they minded going into another room so that these two Polish boys could be together.

'Sometimes RAF officers who had done too many flying hours without a break were brought into the hospital for a rest period. They would be given an injection that would put them out for three or four days. When they came round they could wander around the hotel, have a swim, or enjoy a walk in the gardens.

The hospital was like a little nation within itself, with its own military police and its own hierarchy. The surgeon on each ward would simply be known as The Chief. Professor Alexander was the head surgeon for the whole region and would visit Gleneagles once a week. The largest suite on the first floor was transformed into Matron's office, the drawing room became the convalescence ward, the Royal Lochnagar Suite was converted into a seven-bed officers' ward, the Glendevon became the skin ward, the ballroom was used for shows by ENSA, and there was a Navy, Army and Air Force Institutes (NAAFI) shop located in the main corridor. The Department of Health supplied iron beds and sheets and the hotel supplied the blankets. Most of the remaining hotel furniture was stored in attic rooms on the fourth floor for the duration of the war. If you opened the door of the rooms there you were hit by the smell of mothballs.'

Miss Noble looked after one Polish sailor who, after the war, married a local girl and now lives in Glasgow. Jan Jurjanowicz remains in Miss Noble's memory for an incident which brought a smile to her face during a time when there wasn't a lot to laugh about. 'One day I was in my room and Jan came in and asked for his friend,' she recalls. 'I replied that his friend had gone out to tea. He went away and then came back a short time later and said, in his broken English, "Me very angry for you. Me *very* angry for you. Nazis come bomb my brother, me very sad. Nazis come bomb Sister [Miss Noble], me very glad!" It made me smile. He was upset because I'd let his friend out for tea and he hadn't gone along with him. He was a very brave man and a real survivor. He was torpedoed twice in the war.'

The foreign patients quickly had to get used to the peculiarities of life in a Scottish hospital. When they arrived, they would find hot-water bottles and nightshirts in their lockers, along with any paperwork relating to their case. This was odd enough, but breakfast was truly bizarre. They thought porridge was a pudding, and simply couldn't fathom why these strange people would want to eat pudding for breakfast.

Yet as with so many situations in wartime, people overlooked their cultural differences and pulled together. Gleneagles soon began to feel like a community for the patients and the nursing staff who looked after them. Since petrol rationing made travel difficult, very few patients had visitors, and on a sunny afternoon they could be found sitting in old-fashioned bathchairs in the garden. The nurses would sit beside them and help them to write long letters home.

SAVED BY THE SURGEON

One of the chief surgeons was a brilliant man called Mr Hendrichesen. Wartime called for a high degree of medical ingenuity and Mr Hendrichesen was not afraid to improvise whenever the occasion called for it. He was also known for his considerable patience. One day, a Mr Mitchell was brought into the hospital with a severely shattered leg. He had been run down by a car and on the x-ray his leg was nothing but a bag of bones. The Chief drew a picture of what he wanted the joiner to make as a splint. It resembled a narrow sledge with slots for the bandages – and it worked. Mr Mitchell was taken to theatre where The Chief carefully put all his bones back in place, and the patient spent a long time with the splint on his leg, which helped the bones knit back together.

A case that would have tested even the most brilliant surgeon was that of Robert. Robert was a soldier who had been out on a practice shooting exercise with his friends. A guard was positioned at the door of each shooting hut to make sure all the bullets were removed from the guns before the soldiers entered the hut. Unfortunately for Robert, one of the guns somehow escaped this check and when his friend jokingly pointed the weapon at him and pulled the trigger a live bullet went straight through Robert's body. He reached Gleneagles soaked in blood, with a gaping hole in his chest. The two wounds, one entry and one exit wound, were treated before infection set in. Robert was lucky that the bullet had missed his heart and lungs, but without the vigilance of the nursing staff, he would not have

MOIRA COWIE

*M*OIRA COWIE was the telephonist at Gleneagles during the war, and worked at the hotel for many years after that.

Moira was seconded to Gleneagles at the tender age of 15 by the General Post Office (GPO), who provided trained staff for Emergency Medical Services Hospitals and for other establishments requiring a telephonist.

She settled in well, although the facilities were basic compared to what is on offer at Gleneagles today. Heated water had to be taken up to the basins in the bedrooms and coal was shunted

up to the hotel. Bathrooms were situated at the end of the corridors and the only rooms with *en suite* bathrooms were the suites themselves – this would remain the case until the hotel was re-opened after the war.

Moira was at the centre of everything, observing all the comings and goings of wartime. 'I would leave the hotel at 4.00 pm after duty,' she recalls, 'and all would be quiet. The following day everyone would be running around because a train had arrived. If you wandered into the front hall on a lovely summer's day and could smell ether, then you knew that it must be operating day. The three surgeons would operate throughout the day.'

She remembers one scene at the beginning of the war which illustrated the hardship of the years to come very well. 'We had a group of guests that had been due to sail upon the Queen Mary from Southampton on the 6th of September 1939. Of course, war broke out on Sunday the 3rd of September, so they were stranded at Gleneagles.

'The day before, one of the guests, an American gentleman, had made a series of urgent phone calls in an attempt to get out of the country.

On the Tuesday, two days after war was declared, I remember him standing in the front hall as the first group of evacuees arrived carrying gas masks. Suddenly he saw what life was going to be like for us.' Mr F D Davies managed to get back to America on the personal recommendation of President Truman. Mr Davies returned to Gleneagles after the war, but he would return to a changed land.

The Gleneagles hospital treated its fair share of celebrity patients, including Stewart Grainger, who helped with the tea trolley, and David Niven, as debonair as an officer in the Black Watch as he was in his films. Moira herself came into contact with a most distinguished young gentleman – John Bowes-Lyon.

One of Moira's jobs was to collect telephone money from the wards. 'The only people who had telephones in their rooms were the officers. They were allowed to make and receive calls but all the other patients had to come downstairs and use the coin box.

'One particular day I was doing my telephone rounds when the sister in charge of the ward said, "While you're at it, go next door to my young man. He's not very well and hasn't had any visitors." The sister was one of those people you meet once in a lifetime – a true professional in every way, and perfect for the job.

'The man had been wounded in Yugoslavia, and he'd been sent home. I was nervous before I went in, and wondered what on earth I was going to say. I knocked and entered the room. I couldn't see his face as the sun was shining in through the window. I was halfway across the room before I realised that he was the Queen's nephew, the Master of Glamis. He was a very handsome young man. I had rehearsed what I was going to say carefully, but it was all to no avail – I dried up.

'He laughed and said, "Do sit down." I managed to say, "Sister's asked me to come in and have a chat with you as you haven't had any visitors." He said, "As you can imagine, visitors are hard to come by with rationing – my family doesn't have petrol to come down this far." He was very relaxed and friendly and we talked away. He told me to come and see him when I was next on the ward, which I did.

'I collected the telephone money and then went to Sister and asked her why she hadn't told me it was John Bowes-Lyon. "It doesn't matter who he is," was her no-nonsense reply, "he needs company like everyone else".

'I remember it was the end of September when he was discharged. He was killed at the end of October.

'He was one of twins. It was a complete tragedy as his twin also died in the war, and lost his wife and child. His death shattered me because he was the first person I'd actually known who had been killed. I was only 15.

'My father was the one who finally brought me back to my senses. He told me that John was the eldest son of a great family who would do their own mourning. It wasn't up to us to do that mourning for them. It was the first time I'd really been aware of the feeling that, whatever the hardships, life simply has to go on.'

survived. 'If he sat up we were afraid he'd haemorrhage; if we laid him down there was the danger of pneumonia. He was in for months, but he survived,' remembers Miss Noble.

Another miraculous survivor was a 14-year old boy, also named Robert, who dreamt of following in his father's footsteps and becoming a sailor. One night, when he was out on Air Raid Precautions duty, clearing the area of dud grenades, he picked up a live grenade and lost all four fingers on one hand. He was admitted to St Andrews Hospital before being transferred to Gleneagles, where the doctors knew of the legendary patience and brilliance of The Chief.

The Chief said to Sister Mary Noble, 'Sister, dear, if we can keep a bone at the end of his last finger then at least he can use that to hold a pencil.'

The nurses had to sterilise a pen, paper and ink, clean Robert's hand and then make a paper pattern of it. He was taken to the operating theatre. The Chief placed Robert's hand on his stomach and cut skin from his tummy. He scraped the muscle off and stitched it along the top of Robert's hand, before bandaging it up. 'We were not allowed to leave him for a single second,' remembers Miss Noble. 'Of course, Robert wasn't able to move his hand, because it was sewn on to his stomach.'

Two weeks later, he was taken back down to theatre. The graft had taken and some healthy pink skin had formed. More skin was then taken from his tummy and sewn along his palm – the blood from his stomach was supplying blood to his hand. The operation had been a success and Robert managed to hold a pencil. But he would never be a sailor.

'I have to admit that I was nearly reduced to tears when little Robert looked at me one day and said sadly, "I thought my fingers would grow back," but we did manage to secure him a shore job with the navy.'

KEEPING UP SPIRITS IN TIMES OF TROUBLE

Life may have been pretty tough during wartime, but people never forgot how to have fun. Miss Noble remembers numerous occasions when her boys would play her up relentlessly. 'The patients were allowed to play cards, but not to gamble. If the ward was quiet we would keep a room aside as a common room where the patients could go and have a chat.

One day when I was passing by I heard money clinking, so I opened the door and said, "If I hear this once again I'll report you all to the major." The major was responsible for discipline and if patients were caught breaking the rules they would be punished by Royal Warrant and lose their pay for a number of days.

51

IN THE CARE
OF FRIENDS
The Gleneagles nurses
were unfailing in the care
they gave to patients.

'Another day I was walking past the common room and things were ominously quiet. At times it was like looking after children – silence invariably spelt mischief! Sure enough, they had made paper money so that they could gamble without making a sound.

'When that particular scam failed, the patients had another idea, and resorted to playing in the grounds. Unfortunately for the patients, the military police were on the case and quickly foiled their plan. They soon realised there was no escape.'

Miss Noble remembers one patient who was extremely difficult and who constantly refused to take his medicine. 'I had to call the major in, and he declared, "You should remember in future that a wish expressed by Sister is to be treated as a command." It was very strict but very fair. We had to have co-operation or the patients would not get better, and there had to be discipline doled out with an equal dose of kindness.'

FRIENDS FOR LIFE

For many of the nurses and patients who worked at Gleneagles, the war was an opportunity to forge strong friendships.

Mary Noble participated in a reunion of nurses at Gleneagles in 1995, where she met up with many of her former colleagues, and another major reunion of soldiers, sailors and other servicemen was held in Perth. Miss Noble, who lives in Perth, was very touched by the affection shown by her local community. 'The

HAPPY REUNION
(left to right) Mrs Betty Padyinka, Miss Mary Noble and Miss Bel Clark, pictured opposite in earlier times, reacquaint themselves.

people of Perth all came out to greet the servicemen and cheer. It was thanks to the Lady Provost of Perth that the occasion took place. The servicemen were all very happy to see how eager the people were to come and thank them for their commitment to fight for Britain.

When war was finally over, the doctors and nurses were transferred to other hospitals and life slowly began to regain its normal rhythm. But trying to recapture the atmosphere of the pre-war days would never be quite as easy as putting the furniture back in its original location. A lot of souls had been damaged by the horrors of war and, not surprisingly, people found it extremely difficult to snap back into the party-going, pleasure-seeking lifestyles they had enjoyed in the carefree pre-Second World War days.

Moira Cowie remembers the celebrations for V-J day, which signalled the final end of a long and hard war. 'You could see bonfires all around the hills, lighting up the skies to celebrate the end of the war. I remember standing alongside the physiotherapist. She said, "Well, we've all been ships that have passed in the night. I wonder where we will be this time next year." It made me realise that life was about to change again.'

And change it did. The Second World War marked a watershed for British society. Social structures, behaviour and lifestyle were forever altered by the experience. The Gleneagles Hotel would have to rise to the challenge, respond to the changing demands of a changed world, and look forward to the challenge of the post-war years.

CHAPTER FOUR

The Post-War Years

So, we'll go no more a roving
So late into the night,
Though the heart be still as loving,
And the moon be still as bright.

FROM 'SO, WE'LL GO NO MORE A ROVING'
LORD BYRON

THE SECOND WORLD WAR transformed people's lives. The hedonistic, trouble-free days of the 1920s and 1930s were long gone. The rich and well connected who would flock to Gleneagles for the whole summer season, and had only to worry their pretty heads about whether they would appear on time for glitzy, ritzy cocktails and sumptuous dinners, were finally forced to confront the unpleasant realities of a bitter war.

After the war, Gleneagles became a rehabilitation centre for miners for several years until The London, Midland and Scottish Railway Company (LMS) asked for the place to be returned to them and converted back to a hotel. Thomas Johnston, Secretary of State for Scotland, formally opened the centre, which was the first of its kind in the industry. Its aim was to 'restore to fitness, in the quickest possible time, miners who have been incapacitated through injury or illness'. Treatment was free and miners' travelling expenses were paid for by the Miners Welfare Commission. By the late 1940s, the centre was not only accepting miners, but treating any person working in industry suffering a disability.

Once the hospital had closed its doors, the transformation back to hotel was remarkably quick. As Telephonist Moira Cowie (see feature, page 50) says, 'The last patients left Gleneagles at the beginning of February 1947 and the hotel was opened at Easter. Most things had been stored on the fourth floor and anything that hadn't been stored was replaced.'

Families across the class divide suffered psychological and physical trauma from the war, as well as financial difficulty. Of course, there were still many very rich people in Britain who had either managed to maintain their fortunes or who had built up

OPPOSITE:
TIME TO PARTY
With the relief of the end
of war came the desire to
celebrate a new future.

their wealth through the conflict, but their lifestyles were not the same as in the pleasure-seeking, pre-war days. The war had taken the edge off having fun, and it was a few years before the familiar Gleneagles names started to appear in the reservations book.

In 1947 Moira, who was still a Department of Health telephonist, officially transferred to working for the LMS hotel group. As the central information point on the telephone exchange, she was in an ideal position to watch the comings and goings of the decorators and soft furnishings experts, as they converted the hospital back into a hotel. Moira would frequently spy a tall, good-looking gentleman who would arrive at the hotel, nod to Moira and then go through to the lounge and play the piano. Naturally, she thought he was going to be the resident pianist. But he had a big surprise in store for her!

'A lot of the time I was alone at the front of the hotel, listening to this man playing the piano,' she says. 'One time I ran round to him and asked if he knew how to play 'Clair de Lune'. He said he did and played it for me. I thought no more of it until we had a big meeting at which all the staff were to be introduced to each other.

'The Head Housekeeper and the person in charge of stores came in, followed by various other heads of departments. Then we were told to stand. This struck me as very odd and I wasn't impressed at being told to stand for staff. Much to my surprise, the last person to enter the room was my pianist. I whispered to one of my colleagues, "That's the pianist." He shook everyone's hand, and when he reached me I said, "Oh yes, you're the pianist." There was complete silence. Then he said, "Yes, I am the pianist, but I am also the general manager of all the LMS hotels." I was so embarrassed! He saw my discomfort and laughed. After that he would always make a reference to 'Clair de Lune' whenever he saw me. It became a standing joke.'

Moira found the change from hospital back to hotel a disturbing one in many ways. 'This business of people getting drunk in the bars, stuffing themselves with food and spending hundreds of pounds on dresses to outshine every other guest at dinner seemed so superficial after the tough times we had just experienced. For the first two or three months I felt as though people were wasting money. I had seen such marvellous things in the hospital. Men who were brought in and not expected to live would go to the operating theatre, lie in their beds for months, and then be discharged and rejoin their regiments within a week. Exhausted flying officers on the brink of collapse would come in for a rest, then go straight back to their squadrons and start flying again. We witnessed tremendous courage. And then I saw people getting dolled up for dinner and spending what I thought was a fortune in the bar and dining room. It left a bitter taste in my mouth.'

Moira must have thought she'd stumbled on to a Hollywood film set. Just a few months previously she'd been surrounded by nurses in crisp, starched uniforms, and sisters with white veils. Now the scenery had changed completely and she found herself dressed in black, as dictated by her role as Head Telephonist in an LMS hotel, and spending her day watching waiters running round with their tailcoats flying at 90 degrees.

RETURN TO NORMALITY
On the outside, little had changed, but it took some time for the Gleneagles staff to make the transition from hospital back to hotel.

Moira couldn't help feeling a certain nostalgia for the lack of hierarchy that had characterised wartime relations, but which seemed to have evaporated with the end of the conflict. 'There was a wonderful freedom amongst the staff during the war. When we were off duty we would all play badminton for hours in the ballroom. It didn't matter if you were the chief accountant, a doctor, or the youngest ward helper – we were all in it together. When Gleneagles reverted to a hotel I found it awkward having to address the Head Housekeeper as Madam, and having to stand up when she came in. I felt that the war years had made those distinctions redundant, yet here we were trying to bring the rigid class divisions back. Wage differentials were created and salaried staff were given different rooms according to their level. I also found it very difficult to adjust to the unsociable hours of hotel life, after having worked from 8.00 am until 4.00 pm throughout the war.'

Later, however, when Moira returned to Gleneagles after her first winter season away, she felt the contrast with the war years less strongly, and realised she was still in love with the hotel – and with her job.

THE 1950s

In the 1950s Gleneagles was still operating as a seasonal hotel, open from April to October and closed during winter. The hotel would always open at noon on the Thursday nearest to the 12th of April, and the guests would fight to be awarded the accolade of 'first through the door'. The General Manager was always on hand to greet and welcome his guests.

The seasonal nature of the hotel presented the management with considerable difficulties, not least the problem of what to do with the staff when the season

PEARL CUMMINGS

PEARL CUMMINGS started as a cleaner at The Gleneagles Hotel in her teens, before joining as a full-time member of staff in 1947. She soon worked her way up to become the Gleneagles seamstress, a job which provided variation and an insight into a more genteel way of life.

The guests would often require Pearl's services for alterations and repairs, or she would simply be asked to keep a family member company while the rest of the family went out for the day. The Baileys were such a case. Pearl looked after their mother. 'She was an elegant old lady, probably in her 70s. I'd get her bath ready and we'd decide what she was going to wear. The family would tell me how much money to give her each day and I would put this, together with a clean handkerchief, in the handbag we'd chosen for her to carry. Then off she'd go in a stylish suit, hat and fur stole. In the afternoon I'd do her laundry and press her clothes, then return in the evening to dress her for dinner.'

Acting as a high class lady's maid was not uncommon for Pearl, neither was acting as keeper of the crown jewels, although she did this unawares. 'Lord and Lady Dovecote used to stay in one of the suites and I'd see to Lady Dovecote's laundry. They rarely went down to the dining room, but always dressed for dinner, with Lady Dovecote resplendent in one of her floaty chiffon negligées. She'd get through three or four of them a night. I had to press them on the bed as, according to Lady

Dovecote, this was the only way to avoid stretching the material.

'Lady Dovecote kept huge trunks in the hall. She would hand me the keys and insist I never let them out of my sight. Naturally, I used to wonder what they contained. One day, she asked if I wanted to look inside. I couldn't resist a peek.

'The trunks had several compartments containing huge, beautiful boxes of solid mahogany, which must have been worth a fortune. When Lady Dovecote opened the boxes I was speechless. I had never seen so many magnificent jewels. She had one huge emerald and diamond necklace, a bracelet and a brooch. I couldn't understand why she didn't keep the jewels in the safe. I was terrified of the responsibility she had bestowed upon me and felt it was unfair. There were always people passing through the hall and a burglar could have easily picked the locks. And the funny thing was, not once did I see her wear any of them!'

The staff may not have been able to compete with the guests in terms of opulence, but their dress regulations were certainly just as formal. The Head Housekeeper would wear black during the day, and long black taffeta at night. Pearl would wear a navy skirt and jacket with a white blouse. The valets would always keep a stock of bow ties, evening shirts and even suits, in case a guest came unprepared for a formal occasion. There was no such thing as dressing informally for dinner.

Pearl stayed on as part of the hotel's skeleton winter staff. This was the time the heavy curtains would be cleaned and repaired. A new pair of ballroom curtains would take three or four months to make – an arduous task, but one which Pearl found pleasurable because of the beautiful silk material she worked with. Pearl's winter working hours were supposed to be from 8.00 am until 5.00 pm, but the bottom line was that she, like all the winter staff, worked until the tasks were completed.

ended, and how to get them back when the new season was about to begin. Staff would transfer to other hotels during the 'closed' season and, not surprisingly, managers of the 'winter' hotels would go to great lengths to persuade their valued staff to stay on once Gleneagles re-opened. Breakfast Chef Norman Brockie spent one winter working in a hotel in the north of Scotland and was told he couldn't return to Gleneagles. When he did return, to visit his friends, the Head Chef put him on the spot and demanded to know why he hadn't wanted to come back!

For Moira, life became a little easier. She was sent to Queens Hotel in Leeds after her first season at Gleneagles, and found she loved the variation between city and country. 'I was in the city during the winter and could go out to the cinema and theatre. Around February I would start counting the days until it was time to return to Gleneagles, and then suddenly it would be springtime. I never really thought of it in terms of being a year older, I just thought of it as another season gone by,' she says.

Sometimes staff arriving from the city hotels for the new season at Gleneagles found it a little difficult to settle and there tended to be a large turnover of staff during the first six weeks, causing managers a headache or two. In the city hotels, guests would check in at 5.00 pm and be gone in the morning, whereas at Gleneagles leisurely, extended stays were the norm. 'I suppose Gleneagles was more like a cruise liner, with a small, closed community where everyone had to learn to get on with each other,' says Moira.

RATIONING

Apart from the psychological adjustments to be made, people also had to get used to more tangible changes in their daily lives during the post-war period. One of these was rationing. The shortage of food meant that even a luxury hotel such as Gleneagles could no longer allow its guests to over-indulge. The menus in the Great Dining Room, which now offered a limited amount of food to guests, were at odds with the luxurious ambience of the hotel.

'At lunch time staff were given their ration of butter for the day,' remembers Moira. 'If you ate it all at once, then that was that. We used to have the butter made into pats so it would last longer. The chefs made up something called 'scudderly' – an oatmeal and meat mix resembling a burger, which was a way of helping the meat go round further. Our meals were always entered in the ration book and we never received an extra morsel of anything.'

59

In compliance with an Order of the Ministry of Food not more than One Dish marked "A" and one marked "B" or alternatively Two Dishes marked "B" and not more than three courses in all may be partaken of at any one meal.

Dejeuner

5/-

B	Hors d'Oeuvre Variés
	Consommé Hélene
	Crème Parmentier
B	Filet de Limande Meu
B	Turbotin à la Russ
B	Filet de Haddock Boi
A	Pilaff de Volaille Orie
A	Quartier d'Agneau
A	Buffet Froid et Sal
	Chou Vert Jardinière
	Pommes Nature - Bou
	Pudding Cabin
	Glace Vanille
	Compôte de Fr
	Flan Parisien

A Service Charge is added to all bil

GLENEAGLES HOTEL 21/7

In compliance with an Order of the Ministry of Food not more than One Dish marked "A" and one marked "B" or alternatively Two Dishes marked "B" and not more than three courses in all may be partaken of at any one meal.

DEJEUNER
5/-
(House Charge 2/-)

B	Hors d'Oeuvre Riche
	Consommé aux Pâtes
	Crème Ambassadeur
	Scotch Broth
B	Macaroni aux Tomates
B	Filet de Limande Niçoise
B	Turbotin Grillé Sauce Diable
B	Suprême de Merlan Italienne
A	Pilaff de Volaille à l'Ancienne
A	Omelette Chasseur
A	Côte de Boeuf Rôti
	Buffet Froid et Salade
	Chou Vert Chou-fleur Polonaise
	Carottes Vichy
	Pommes Nature - Parmentier - Purée
	Entremets Divers
	Fromage

A Service Charge is added to all bills in lieu of gratuities.

GLENEAGLES HOTEL 20/7/47 PERTHSHIRE

THE GUESTS RETURN

Gradually, the famous faces of the pre-war years began to return to Gleneagles, as people started to pick up the thread of their lives again. Lady Dorothy MacMillan (wife of the then Prime Minister, Harold MacMillan), Sir Leslie and Lady Gamage and others made their way to their favourite Scottish hotel, and life there began to recapture its old rhythm. In the days before the package tour holiday, travel was still very much for the privileged few, and speed was not the primary concern when foreign holidays were arranged. People would take one train from Scotland to London, a second from London to Calais, and then whatever form of travel was required to reach their holiday destination. The journey could quite easily take three days and the travel was considered part of the holiday.

Gleneagles rediscovered a quiet, measured pace of life. 'If I was on duty at 7.00 am, I'd walk past the bakehouse and know that the baker had been there since 4.00 am, and that he'd clock off at 12 noon,' says Moira. 'The restaurant had strict opening hours for breakfast, lunch and dinner. In the high season (July to the beginning of September), the dining room would be open until midnight or 1.00 am. A band played in the lounge from 9.00 pm until midnight and as soon as we heard the band strike up 'I'll see you in my dreams', everybody who worked at the front of the hotel knew it was 11.55 pm and time to hand over to the night porter and go to bed. The night porter dealt with everything from that point on, unless any guests had asked for a meal to be served in their room, in which case we had to call a waiter, as only the waiters were allowed to serve meals. Last orders were at 9.30 pm – any later and you had to have the meal brought to your room. Rules were strict and unusual requests were not automatically catered for as they are today.'

The telephone exchange was Moira's own little kingdom and Auchterarder 70 was the magic code. It would be years before an automatic system was installed, so all the calls went through Moira. Consequently, she got to know the guests very well, and they would often come and see her on arrival and on departure. Moira was particularly fond of Lady Dorothy MacMillan. 'Lady Dorothy would always travel on the overnight train from London at 7.00 am on the 13th or 14th of August. She would be met at the station and be driven to the hotel, then she'd have breakfast and wash before coming to see me. We'd sit and chat until the Head Porter arrived to tell her that her car was at the front. Every time she visited she'd say, "You're still here then?" and I'd reply, "Oh yes. I'm in here with the bricks." We'd have a chat and then she'd be off further north to see her sister. She always came dressed in an old brown skirt, a pink knitted jumper and a brown knitted cardigan that my mother wouldn't even have been seen in to do the gardening, but she was so nice and friendly it didn't seem to matter. She just seemed like an ordinary person. I had no idea who her husband was.

'When Prime Minister Harold MacMillan himself came to stay at Gleneagles security was intense, with constant checks by police and sniffer dogs. The place was a hive of activity when Lady Dorothy walked in. "Just checking you're still here," she said. "For goodness' sake, Lady Dorothy. What a day to choose!" I said. "The

FRANK O'DONNELL

*P*EARL CUMMING'S MALE COUNTERPART at the hotel was Frank O'Donnell. Frank joined the hotel as a valet in 1960, retired in 1992, and then came back to work for the golf club.

Frank had previously worked for a Glasgow tailor and at a clothing factory, so was ideally suited to the demands of the job of valet. While Pearl attended to the dress requirements of the ladies, Frank made sure the gentlemen's attire was washed, dried, pressed and laid out to wear. He started off on the third floor, and soon took charge of all three floors. One of his fellow valets had previously worked for a Lord, and was so dedicated to his job that he was up polishing shoes at 6.00 am! Frank had to unpack the guests' clothes, and then lay out all the different changes of clothes the guests would require during the course of the day. The Dormy Clubhouse had no drying room, so all the golf clothes had to be brought back to the hotel to be dried as well.

'In the morning we'd collect everything to be washed and cleaned. We'd lay out a change of clothes for when the gentleman returned from golf, and then lay out his formal clothes for a glittering evening in the ballroom,' Frank remembers. 'We'd work late into the night, drying and cleaning the garments for the following morning.'

Like Pearl, Frank had his fair share of famous names to attend to.

When the late King Hussein of Jordan and Queen Noor spent their honeymoon at Gleneagles, Frank had the job of seeing to all the laundry and cleaning requirements of the 40 staff and bodyguards that made up the royal entourage. Similarly, when Secretary of State James Nott stayed at the hotel, he was so impressed with Frank's service that Frank received a recommendation from the Home Office for his work.

Frank took pride in the work he carried out at Gleneagles and always looks back on his time of service with fondness and satisfaction.

Prime Minister's coming today and the place is full of security officers." "Don't move," she said, "I must bring my husband to meet you." The Prime Minister walked in and Lady Dorothy introduced me as, "the girl who's in with the bricks". He laughed and lifted his hat, by which time I was sitting with my mouth open like a goldfish. I did manage to say, "No wonder you're not worried by security, Lady Dorothy – you're the cause of it". She laughed and they left. I was amazed. I had no idea she was Lady Dorothy MacMillan. The Head Porter thought I was a fool, but I just never got round to asking her what her second name was.

'About an hour later, Lady Dorothy rang through and asked me if I could contact Drummond Castle and find out at what time the MacMillans were expected for dinner. When I called I spoke to a woman who rambled on and on about how difficult it was to get good staff these days, and a whole host of other worries and dramas. "Yes, it must be awful," I sympathised, while at the same time trying to answer the other calls that were coming through, as I was alone on duty. I had called her at 6.15 pm and at 6.55 pm she finally hung up, with the words, "I'd love to see them at 7.00 pm." I realised I'd been speaking to Lady Ancaster herself.

I called Lady Dorothy and apologised for not getting back to her earlier. She just laughed and said, "Did she keep you talking?" Lady Dorothy found it very amusing. She was always so relaxed and easy to talk to.'

A NEW ERA

In 1957 Dennis Aldridge became General Manager of The Gleneagles Hotel. He was known for his immaculate appearance and ran the hotel according to a strict but fair regime. He worked within the LMS hotel group, and had met many famous people through his work. Some of them followed him into his new hotel.

Dennis Aldridge knew Bob Hope from the Central Hotel in Glasgow and from the North British Hotel (now Balmoral) in Edinburgh. When Mr Hope arrived at Gleneagles, he instantly recognised Mr Aldridge. 'Is my laundry back yet?' he quipped.

Mr Aldridge has happy memories of the famous American comedian. 'Bob Hope was a very good golfer and he always played to an audience. The audience was his lifeline. He was here once when Rita Hayworth and a friend were staying. When he walked out on to the first tee a crowd had gathered, so he looked around and said, "I think we have some of Rita's leftovers."

'He was always ready with a joke. I remember being the butt of one once myself when he was speaking at a fundraising dinner, and describing the time he first met me. "Mr Aldridge is debonair, suave and well dressed," he said. "We met and he showed me to my room. He left me and then returned a quarter of an hour

HENRY COTTON
One of the finest golf players Britain has ever produced was a famous visitor at The Gleneagles Hotel in the 1950s.

later. He then demanded, 'Hope, have you got a woman in there?' I said 'no' so he threw one in!"

Henry Cotton, one of the world's greatest golfers, was another famous visitor. His wife, Toots, was a South American firecracker. One day, having consumed a large amount of Krug champagne at dinner, Henry and Toots were clearly beginning to get on each other's nerves, so Henry left the dining room and went into the lounge, where an orchestra was playing. He asked the wife of one of the co-sponsors of a golf tournament to dance. Shortly after, Toots came into the lounge, walked on to the dance floor, separated Henry and his dance partner, and slapped Henry across the face.

Henry calmly apologised to his dance partner, went to Reception, asked for another room and left by taxi early the following morning. Mr Aldridge gave strict instructions to Moira Cowie that nobody was to make a call out of the hotel, and that she was to be wary of any call into the hotel. He was adamant the press would not hear about the incident.

Predictably, it didn't take long for word to get out. Jack Buchan, a well-known Perth-based journalist, was woken at 1.30 am by half of Fleet Street and told to go and investigate. He was not amused but off he went. 'I dressed, combed my hair, got into the car, rammed my foot down hard on the accelerator and set up at top speed for the hotel.'

Buchan arrived at the hotel and tried to mingle with the concierge staff, as they weren't in tails and would, he hoped, provide a camouflage. But soon the redoubtable Mr Aldridge appeared with two 'heavies'. He invited Mr Buchan to his office for a pot of tea and sandwiches. There followed a ridiculous conversation in which pleasantries masked the fact that both sides were quite clearly aware of what the other was up to. 'Thank you, Mr Aldridge, but I was making for home and I spotted the lights, you know, and just thought I'd pop in,' said Buchan. 'But you simply cannot leave us so hurriedly, Mr Buchan,' said Mr Aldridge. 'I'm so delighted to see you – such a long time. How are you? Your family? Your job?'

And so it went on. Dennis Aldridge kept the journalist in the hotel until he was sure that Fleet Street would have gone to bed. At 4.30 am Jack Buchan was allowed to leave. He left without his scoop, but it would not be too long before it all came to light.

The next day came the problem of how to get Toots out of the hotel. Mr Aldridge was still playing a cat and mouse game with the press. 'We had wanted to smuggle Toots on to the sleeper, but a picture had been taken of her walking through the train corridors. Some days later, Henry Cotton arrived back on the sleeper train. The press knew of his arrival, and were waiting for him on the platform. Henry knew exactly how to handle the press, and said simply, "If you're married to a South American you can expect to have an exciting marriage." And that was that.

Mr Aldridge was also witness to a disaster in the hotel that eventually turned into a triumph. He describes the scene: 'We were having an end-of-conference dinner in the Glendevon room. It had been a difficult conference and the atmosphere was somewhat strained. Anyway, we went ahead with our haggis ceremony. The haggis procession, consisting of a piper, followed by the chef with the cleanest whites, who held the haggis, and the Head Waiter, who performed a juggling act with two bottles of whisky, marched into the room. As the procession reached the dance floor, the chef tripped and the haggis flew into the air and landed with a great thud – then the Head Waiter fell on top of the chef. At first the piper didn't realise what had happened, but when he turned round and surveyed the scene, there was a silence broken only by the sound of pipes coming to a grinding halt. It was the ultimate icebreaker and, to the delight of the head of the conference, everyone began talking and laughing with each other.'

There were other occasions when things didn't quite go to plan. When a major cinematographic conference was being held near Gleneagles, its five or six hundred attendees would all take their meals at the hotel. Mr Aldridge remembers a particularly problematic day. 'The Staff Manager came to me and explained we had a strike on our hands – the waiters were refusing to serve lunch. The Staff Manager had been cutting down on overtime and everyone was up in arms about it. I went to talk to the staff and agreed to look into it, but that it wouldn't look too good on their CVs if they had a strike record. Needless to say they all went back to work.'

Dennis Aldridge's reign as General Manager was certainly one marked by a fair amount of conflict. The Haldanes were a family who had lived in the estate of Gleneagles for generations and who were sick and tired of hearing The Gleneagles Hotel referred to simply as 'Gleneagles', which they regarded as their territory. A kind of running battle ensued between the Haldanes and the hotel. Mr Haldane demanded that the Post Office deliver all letters marked simply 'Gleneagles' to him. He would then keep them for a while before passing them on to the hotel, with a red line under the word 'Gleneagles' and the word 'Hotel' added to the address.

Mr Aldridge has happier memories of the time Prime Minister MacMillan and Lady Dorothy visited the hotel. Lady Dorothy was determined Mr Aldridge's three children would meet the Prime Minister, and this was duly arranged. Harold MacMillan was in jovial mood. He had his detective alongside him and he turned to Dennis Aldridge, and said, 'You know, Aldridge, this detective chap of mine is brilliant – a crack shot. I have no doubt that if someone took a shot at me he could kill the assailant without any problem. The only thing is, the assailant would have shot me first!'

THE 1960s

As the hotel moved into the 'swinging sixties', the social class barriers began to break down a little and the atmosphere at Gleneagles became more relaxed. However, efficiency and the personal touch were still valued and the staff were expected to maintain a certain formality.

Moira Cowie's GPO training stipulated that all calls had to be answered within five seconds. Any longer was simply unacceptable. It was a struggle to keep to these exacting standards during the early evening peak time – 6.00 pm was when the cheap rate came in, and all the guests made phone calls before going down for drinks and then dinner. Moira came to know what a guest's requirements would

BOBBY WRIGHT – BALANCING THE BOOKS

BOBBY WRIGHT worked as a book-keeper at Gleneagles from 1955 until 1991. In the days before the computer was king, huge ledgers would be used on which to record all the financial information, and balancing the books was an enormous and cumbersome task.

'We had to balance the page from left to right and from top to bottom,' he explains. 'We used to have 150 bedrooms on one page and then the rest of the hotel on the next page. Everything had to be carried forward. The previous day's business had to be closed by 10.00 am in the morning and the controllers would then have to get the cheques and payments ready to balance the books. The controllers worked in five-day shifts and everything was checked on an additional night shift.

'We often worked late into the night to keep everything up-to-date. If entries got behind then it was pretty disastrous – the whole book would fail to balance and it would take hours to sort out.'

After a spell as a book-keeper, Bobby moved on to wages. This was equally complex as, again, everything had to be worked out manually. With just two people working on wages, and most of the staff paid weekly from time sheets, it was a constant struggle to keep up. The wages were paid by British Transport Hotels, whose headquarters were St Pancras Chambers in London, so special forms had to be filled out if anyone was off sick, and the wages re-calculated.

In 1981, privatisation came and Gleneagles Hotels plc was born. Yet this didn't make it easier for the wages staff. 'When Gleneagles was still an independent unit, it was easy to work out the wages. If someone left, we'd know how much they were owed within half an hour. But when we had to process things through the new limited company, it became a lot more difficult to recover money.'

Like many numerate people, Bobby took easily to computers, and was used to working a keyboard. Initially, processing one invoice would require pushing 11 buttons, which he could do in 23 seconds. Bobby was just as quick when the system was computerised.

Bobby's job was not without its frustrations, but he still loves the hotel. 'Gleneagles has always been rather like a family concern,' he explains. 'If you were working in one department, and needed to go and consult a member of staff in another department, then you would more than likely know the person you were going to see. It made it so much easier to get co-operation from people, and for everyone to work together happily and in harmony.'

be without having to ask. 'When the switchboard lit up you'd know which room it was, who was in it and exactly what they wanted,' she explains. 'Sometimes a guest would say to me, "Could you get my wife on the line, please?" They wouldn't always leave a room number – you just got to know voices and the requests that went with them.

'Sean Connery would visit just about every year. He'd phone from almost every part of the world. He'd always ask me how I was, and we'd have a chat about what the golfing conditions were like and so on. It was wonderful privilege to have that kind of personal contact, but we were careful not to overstep the boundaries of formality.

'We never called guests by their first name, and the manager would always address me as 'Miss Cowie' when I was on duty. I hated it when, later on, I had to wear a name badge with 'Moira' on it. I believed formality and discipline were appropriate in the environment we worked in and I felt it was important to know how to talk to people without fawning, and without being too friendly. The Duke of Marlborough might pop in for a chat between dances, but that didn't necessarily mean it was acceptable to converse with him if he passed you in the corridor half an hour later.'

Linkman Billy Lynch started at Gleneagles as a pageboy in 1961 and has vivid memories of the hotel in the 1960s. 'We worked two shifts – from 8.00 am to 8.00 pm, and then from 8.00 pm to 8.00 am. We worked six days a week, had fifteen minutes for breakfast and thirty minutes for lunch. If you were lucky you got a two-hour break between shifts. If you were unlucky then you worked straight through. We had two weeks holiday a year. We were paid two pounds ten shillings a week and thought we were millionaires. Food and accommodation were provided and so our wages were pocket money.'

Billy would stand proudly in the hall wearing his little pageboy hat and white gloves. His duties were to deliver messages and bouquets to the rooms, and go to the dining room if there was a phone call for one of the guests, then escort the guest to the nearest phone. Today, messages are taken by computer and simply placed on the voicebox mail system. Newspapers are placed outside the rooms, whereas in Billy's day the papers were usually slid under the door. If they were too bulky, then the pageboy would take the pass key and lay them just inside the room.

After a year as a pageboy, Billy became a junior porter and started his ascent up the Gleneagles ladder. As junior porter, he had to clean the brass, clean the windows, carry luggage to and from the rooms and perform all the general tasks assigned to him by the Head Porter.

GHOSTS

Like many of the Gleneagles staff, Billy worked through the winter. He would pace the eerily quiet hotel on the night shift during the long hours of darkness, and sense strange, ghostly presences. He was already familiar with some of the stories and legends associated with the hotel and on those long nights, was forced to take such stories seriously.

'In the winter, when the hotel was closed, there'd be no carpets down, no central heating and no lights on. You'd walk around two or three times a night to check the keys [for insurance purposes]. Clocks with keys in them were located at certain points along the corridors. You'd turn the key and that would be the signal to the insurance company that a particular part of the building had been checked. The fourth floor was where I would hear most of the strange noises. I could feel a presence everywhere, as if someone was walking behind me, but on the fourth floor it was at its most intense. I'd turn round, but there'd be no-one there.'

FRANCIS BROWN – THE PINEAPPLE KING

ONE OF THE GREAT characters to visit the hotel in the 1960s was Francis Brown, the Pineapple King. He came from Hawaii with his consort, Miss Love. The Pineapple King had Scottish ancestors and his father had made a fortune by discovering how to tin pineapple. He would bring two Cadillacs with him, with two spare wheels at the rear.

The Pineapple King was a very generous man, and very fond of the Gleneagles staff. He set up an annual football competition between the staff teams from two local hotels – The Gleneagles Football Team took on the team from the Central in Glasgow in the quest for the glory of lifting The Hawaiian Cup.

Billy Lynch remembers Mr Brown very well. 'The football match was held on the staff recreation ground,' recalls Billy. 'The winning team would get a gold watch, and the runners-up would get exactly the same! Then there would be a banquet in the hotel in the evening. Mr Brown did that every year. One year it would be at Gleneagles, and the next year at the Central in Glasgow.

'That was the Pineapple King. He was a real character and an incredibly generous and thoughtful man. If he went down into the village for a drink one evening, then he would make sure that everyone in the pub was bought one too. He'd simply leave £50 behind the bar and instruct the bar staff to keep topping up everybody's glass.

'The Pineapple King remained a bachelor as it was considered unacceptable for him to marry his Hawaiian lady, Miss Love, but they were always together.'

On a number of occasions, guests staying in a room on the third floor claimed to have seen a little boy and a little girl, dressed in 18th-century costume, and standing at the foot of the bed.

Warming to his theme, Billy continues, 'The story of the two children did not surprise me in the slightest. The Gleneagles building was not very old at the time these sightings occurred, but you could certainly feel a presence there. Perhaps it was even a hark back to the days of Bonnie Prince Charlie and his troops in Auchterarder. I could always sense the presence very strongly by the back staircase, opposite the Barony room. The Barony room was used as the operating theatre in the Second World War.

'Comedian Jim Davidson swore he had seen a ghost in his room when he was staying at the hotel. When he returned a year or so later, I said to him, "Your pal's upstairs waiting for you." He turned to his companion and said, "Didn't I tell you Billy would back my story?" He never went back into the room. I have to say I had no difficulty in believing his story – I genuinely think there are ghosts around the place.'

LABOURS OF LOVE

If some staff recall eerie relationships with ghostly presences, others associate the hotel with far happier relations, and many Gleneagles workers have found romance within the hotel walls. Breakfast Chef Norman Brockie met his wife Christine at the hotel. He was working in the kitchens, and she was in charge of room service on the second floor. Norman had set his heart on the pretty, vivacious girl who

GENERAL MANAGERS
at GLENEAGLES

1924	F C Fisher
1932-34	C Pittolo
1935-37	R Nichols
1938-39	C Pittolo
1947-48	E R Cottet
1949-51	F R Collins
1952-54	H A Berry
1955	D A V Aldridge
1956	H A Berry
1957-63	D A V Aldridge
1964	I M Jack
1965	I M Jack
	V P R Woodcock
1966	V P R Woodcock
1967-69	D A V Aldridge
1970-82	J K S Bannatyne MBE
1984-88	P J Lederer
1988-92	V Sirotkin
1992-98	P J Lederer ★
1998-	George Graham

★ *General Manager and Managing Director*

would appear in the kitchen to collect something for one of the guests. At first Christine didn't notice Norman, but he refused to give up and his persistence eventually paid off when they got together at one of the staff dances. They were engaged on Burns Night 1964 and married on the 27th of March 1965.

Norman, an Aberdonian by birth, discovered later that his mother-in-law had also been a Gleneagles girl. Christina McRostie, who was born in 1908, had been the first girl caddy, working at Gleneagles just after the end of the First World War, when the golf courses were inaugurated. Christina, who is still as bright as a button, remembers those days fondly. 'I was a ten-year-old girl with a long, blonde plait, dressed in plus fours. I knew every hole on the courses. I loved The Queen's Course and The King's was very good as well. I enjoyed caddying, although I never had time to learn to play the game. Caddies could make a lot of money in those days – we were paid two shillings a round and could get half a crown or one shilling as a tip. Summer was good, and when the snow came in winter we used to skate on the pond and hold curling competitions.'

Valet Frank O'Donnell was another member of staff who found love at the hotel. Frank met his wife when she was working as a housekeeper on the first floor, and they went on to have three children. The O'Donnell family hasn't strayed too far from Frank's spiritual home – the family have a house near The Monarch's golf course.

Gleneagles also gave seamstress Pearl Cummings a second chance of happiness. When her first husband died, she was left to bring up three small children. Five years later, she met and married her second husband, who was in charge of the heating at the hotel.

THE 1970s

The 1970s saw the arrival of James Bannatyne as the new General Manager of Gleneagles. He would remain at the helm until 1982.

Mr Bannatyne's association with the hotel had in fact begun many years earlier when, in 1948, he was employed by Gleneagles as a kitchen clerk. From there he went on to the Caledonian Hotel in Edinburgh to do his waiter training, before returning to Gleneagles as Senior Assistant Manager in 1953, which was Queen Elizabeth II's coronation year.

Fifty years on, James Bannatyne's memories of his first impression of Gleneagles are still vivid. 'I thought it was a wonderful place. The London, Midland and Scottish Railway Company owned many hotels, but Gleneagles was the *crème de la crème*. Rationing meant the hotel was really just turning over at that time, but we

survived because staff salaries were next to nothing and the room charge relatively high. We were making some money, but things didn't really take off in terms of profit until we made our move into the conference business.'

The conference business started to grow in the 1960s and 1970s, but the double blow of VAT and high inflation meant that rates for conference facilities were forced to rise by 25 per cent and this, combined with a drop in the US dollar, meant that initially, it was a slow growth.

The 1970s will be remembered by many as the decade of strikes, and Gleneagles did not escape the effects of worker discontent. Mr Bannatyne recalls, 'We were living in an exciting new era. We expected such a lot. But then the strikes started and this affected the economy. We were doing very good business up until the dockers' strike of 1970, but then when television stations started showing pictures of empty supermarket shelves we began to see wholesale cancellations. A big conference of delegates from France cancelled as the delegates believed there would be no food available in Britain! The dustmen's strike during the 'winter of discontent' in 1979 had similar negative effects. We were well away from it, but it affected our business and made foreigners reluctant to come to the U.K.'

In 1977 The Commonwealth Prime Ministers' Conference brought considerable prestige to the hotel. The agreement on racism in sport that was signed at the conference is still referred to as 'The Gleneagles Agreement'. 'Our biggest worry was that Ugandan leader Idi Amin would be attending,' recalls Mr Bannatyne. 'He had every right to do so, of course, but nobody wanted him there. We felt nervous right up until the last minute, when it was confirmed that he would not be turning up.'

The aim of the conference weekend was to get the leaders away from the conference table and allow them to interact in individual groups. There was a certain amount of tension in the air.

JIM BANNATYNE

PRIME MINISTERS' CONFERENCE
In 1977 prime ministers from around the world gathered at The Gleneagles Hotel. India's Prime Minister Desai (left) and Britain's Jim Callaghan were among them.

69

'Apartheid was still a major issue and you could sense a fair bit of bitterness between the black and white attendees,' says Mr Bannatyne. 'The weather was awful and the ministers all arrived with long faces – it was hardly the most auspicious start. We had to clear the hotel of guests, MI5 came along and examined the staff records, and we were all given badges. The SAS, so I believe, were not far away, with all the latest electronic gadgets at the ready so they could hear a rabbit sniffing in the undergrowth.

'Meal times were tricky, as quite a few of the delegates had special dietary requirements. The Indian Prime Minister, Mr Desai, was a strict vegetarian. He would only eat fruit and drink warm milk. We gave him his own bowl of fruit. The other Prime Ministers ate their first course and then made inroads into Mr Desai's fruit. He gave me such a sad look, as if to say, "that's all I have," so we quickly got him another bowlful. Mr Fraser, the Australian premier, who at six feet six inches tall required a special extension for his bed, insisted on being served haggis. We did as he asked, but tried to be diplomatic with the other guests, who objected to haggis for religious or dietary reasons.

'In the end, the conference went very well. We managed to give each prime minister a suite, although we only just made it on the furniture front. Fortunately, I had a three-piece suite stored in the hotel attic, waiting for my new house in Auchterarder to be completed. I was able to bring it down and put it in Prime Minister Jim Callaghan's suite. When my wife asked if she could see Mr Callaghan's suite I held my breath, but luckily she failed to recognise the sofa and chairs, which I was very relieved about!'

Throughout the 1970s Gleneagles continued to play host to film stars and major celebrities. Seamstress Pearl Cummings has strong memories of one encounter. 'The Gleneagles rule was that celebrities were left alone unless they asked for someone to assist them. Christopher Lee would always ask for me when he came to stay at the hotel. He was fond of buying tartan trousers and he would give these to the valet, with the command, "Take these to Pearl, she knows what to do with them." The valet used to try to make me take the trousers back to Mr Lee when I'd finished the alterations, but I was always reluctant. He gave me the creeps in those films of his. One time, however, I gave in. Mr Lee was staying in room 83. When you opened the door to the corridor you were greeted by a long, dark hallway. I should have put the light on, but I didn't. I knocked on the door and out he came. He was very nice but those eyes terrified me. I said to the valet, "Don't you ever send me down there again." And he didn't.'

THE 1980s

It was, appropriately, during the Thatcher reign of the 1980s that Gleneagles looked to privatisation to revitalise both its finances and its image.

A new company was formed to buy Gleneagles, together with the Caledonian and North British Hotels in Edinburgh. This company was Gleneagles Hotels plc. It received an investment injection of over £5 million, intended to secure the hotel's future, and the management decided to keep the hotel open all year round.

The hotel pulled out all the stops to ensure maximum security when it hosted the NATO conference in 1981. The security arrangements for The Commonwealth Prime Ministers' Conference four years previously paled in comparison. The area was sealed off and all flying in the area was forbidden. Even Ginger, the hotel cat, was given his own pass so he could move through security with out being questioned!

Peter Lederer, the current Managing Director of The Gleneagles Hotel, was brought in by the privatised company to act as General Manager and oversee the operation of taking the rather tired hotel into the 20th century and beyond. At the time, Peter Lederer was a successful 33-year-old working and living in Canada. When the call up came, the challenge of revitalising such a fantastic establishment proved too enticing to resist. Peter was quite happy with his life in Canada – in fact the opportunity to manage The Gleneagles Hotel was just about the only thing that would have persuaded him to return to Britain. He took up his new post in 1984.

'Investment in the late 1970s had been virtually non-existent and when I came to the hotel the place was in a rather sorry state, and living largely on its reputation. The first thing we did was to create The Country Club,' says Peter. 'It opened in 1982.

'Our main challenge was to find a way of persuading people that they wanted to spend the winter here in Scotland. We knew that we needed to offer alternatives

SHOOTING STARS
Steven Spielberg, Sean Connery and Harrison Ford at a Rolex/Jackie Stewart Celebrity Challenge event.

71

ROOM TO RELAX

One of the goals of any hotel is to provide an environment where the guests feel relaxed and at home. The Gleneagles Hotel is no exception.

to golf, and so we began to look at various other activities. The first facility to be constructed was the Shooting School. We felt that shooting, which was an outdoor activity traditionally popular with the type of guest who frequented Gleneagles, would be a good sport to offer.

'We put a lot of effort into sales and marketing, with events such as our Zandra Rhodes fashion show, and we got falconry experts Steve and Emma Ford to hold falconry weekends, which proved very popular. We also organised business weekends hosted by celebrity agent Mark McCormack, and we set up The Equestrian Centre.

'Attracting the younger business crowd was essential. The 1980s saw an increase in the disposable income of young people and it was up to us to find a way of capitalising on that. Equally, however, people were more discerning as to how they would spend their leisure time – they wanted to be entertained and they wanted to be the first to try out new sports and activities. We had to ensure that the new-look Gleneagles was in tune with the lifestyle our guests aspired to. Once the younger crowd realised that the hotel was a relatively relaxed establishment, and no longer slave to the rules and regulations of previous years, they soon began to make Gleneagles their home.

'Golf at Gleneagles was in need of an injection of excitement, so we decided to organise our now famous pro-celebrity tournaments. The tournaments were an immediate success, and were well attended by a host of VIPs and celebrities. Jackie Stewart himself organised the Rolex/Jackie Stewart Celebrity Challenge, which

BILL McFARLAN – THE MEDIA MAN

THE technological developments that have taken place during the lifetime of Gleneagles have been astounding and in the 1990s growth has been unprecedented. At the opening of the hotel in 1924, the guests were entranced by the novelty of the first radio broadcast from the Highlands, when the Henry Hall concert was played to a UK audience. Since then, digital television has arrived, man has walked on the moon, mobile phones have become *de rigueur* and Concorde gets us from London to New York in less time than it takes to drive from London to Edinburgh. We are used to being able to communicate instantly with the rest of the world, and the rest of the world is used to being able to communicate instantly with us.

Technological advancement brings its own demands and pressures and the man in charge of helping Gleneagles communicate successfully with the rest of the world is Bill McFarlan, co-founder of The Broadcasting Business.

Bill, a well-known former sports and news presenter for the BBC, knows that an international hotel must communicate effectively with the

world, and is working to demystify the media in the eyes of the Gleneagles staff. 'A lot of people are scared of the media,' he explains. 'We want to remove the fear and transform the staff into media experts themselves. Gleneagles is famous throughout the world, and attracts great interest. I have sent videos of the hotel to many countries. Often television or radio programmes are looking for an expert on cookery, golf, fitness or falconry. Tom Watson, the starter on The King's Course, appeared recently on BBC Breakfast News, talking about the hotel.

'My job is to ease communication between Gleneagles and the media,' says Bill. 'The stories are there, I just have to

unlock the process and let both sides bring out the best in each other. Television link-ups mean you can become an instant star, or an instant disaster, and it's up to me to train the staff so that they know how to be the former, rather than the latter.

'In the 1970s, the Gleneagles management would refuse to have dealings with the media except through a spokesperson. Now people want to see the characters and experts in person. I believe that if companies are to survive in the 21st century, they must be empowered to speak to all forms of the media with confidence.'

Bill is also a regular guest of the hotel, having brought his wife and children to Gleneagles on many occasions. His relationship with the hotel is based on mutual respect and mutual advantage. But it is hard work that has made Bill the number one choice for media training. 'Personality wins business, but character keeps it,' he says. 'To envisage the future you have to take a big step towards it. Gleneagles always wants to go beyond its previous best, so it is constantly at the cutting edge of innovation.'

73

attracted considerable media attention and brought in good business for The Gleneagles Hotel.'

The 1980s was also the decade the hotel began to expand into Europe and today 12 per cent of its business is with its European neighbours. Golf is still a sport in its infancy in France, Italy, Germany and Austria, and these countries should provide an important growth area. America is an important market for Gleneagles and continues to develop.

In the 1990s, the management began to look at updating the golfing facilities at Gleneagles. 'We needed a new championship course,' says Peter Lederer. 'The men's

game had moved on in terms of technology and equipment and so we asked Jack Nicklaus to design a new course. The result is The Monarch's. The Monarch's Course is our future.'

The £2.7 million redevelopment of The Club has also been a huge success. Peter Lederer's ambition to attract outside members as well as hotel guests to The Club has largely been realised, and the new Club now has over 1500 members and offers a wide range of social activities.

When Peter became Managing Director, George Graham took over as General Manager. George joined Gleneagles in 1981 and found the hotel 'somewhat starchy, like a worn old slipper – comfy, but with holes in the toe'. He remembers when the leisure club was the old garage, housing the guests' cars, the chauffeurs and the kennels for the gun dogs. 'The changing rooms were built on what was one side of the garage and the pool on the other. There was a small gym on the left of the pool. The pool was exposed to viewers on their exercise bikes and the bikes would get rusty from the moisture from the pool. In the winter the fog would swirl around inside the building. Updating the leisure facilities was one of the first tasks we tackled.'

Another priority was to convert the staff bedrooms on the fourth floor into guest bedrooms. This was a complex affair as the existing pipework meant the corridor had to be moved a couple of metres, but it gave the hotel another 30 bedrooms, which were considered essential if Gleneagles was to compete in the ever-growing conference business.

George Graham describes the current Gleneagles style as an 'art deco feel ... like that of a luxury liner'. George has done his research and knows what the guests want. 'We know they want big showers with good water pressure,' he explains. 'They want space for the sake of space. We want them to open the bathroom door and be knocked out by the feeling of space. That's why we've put baths in the middle of the bathrooms in some cases, or created space by knocking two rooms into one. Some of the new rooms have wooden floors, with special textiles and metals on the walls.'

Today the hotel has an average 35 per cent return rate among guests. Staying at Gleneagles is still a special experience. As George Graham says, 'Gleneagles touches the heart. It gets inside your soul and becomes part of you. I still get a shiver down my spine when I arrive in the morning. It's more than just a place of work, and that's why the staff often return here after having gained additional experience elsewhere. We have a very friendly culture, and we don't get tied up in playing politics. We all care about one another, and we care about the future of the hotel.'

75

SWIMMING IN SPLENDOUR
The magnificent new redeveloped swimming pool and Jacuzzi.

CHAPTER FIVE

The Gleneagles Experience

'I'd like time to stop right now, because I could stay in this place forever.'
Colin Freedman's son Scott – lying in the grass near the 3rd tee of The King's
Course, gazing at the Ochil Hills

*'I love the computers and seeing what goes on in the kitchens. The food is
the best, I could live here and be looked after like this forever.'*
Terry Waldron's nephew, Oliver Hairs

OB HOPE, one of the world's greatest entertainers, is
one person who has been captivated by what can only
be described as The Gleneagles Experience. The
Gleneagles Experience is unique. It enters the soul of the casual
visitor and makes it impossible for him or her to stay away from
the 'Highland Palace' for too long. Bob Hope first walked out on
to The King's Course in the 1950s and thus began a lifelong love
affair with Gleneagles. An extremely talented golfer, he was still
making the pilgrimage to the hotel in the 1990s, by then well into
his nineties himself. In that time he has made many friends.

Linkman Billy Lynch is a firm fan of the famous comedian
and has many fond memories of both Bob Hope and his fellow
entertainer, Bing Crosby. 'Bob Hope and Bing Crosby were
brilliant people. About 10 or 15 years ago, Bob Hope sent me his
book, in which he'd written, "Thanks for the memory, Billy." He
always remembers me. He's a marvellous man.'

Even in old age, Bob Hope entrances the people he meets.
Billy remembers when Bob Hope walked into the dining room
and the pianist started to play 'Thanks for the Memory'. The whole
room stood up and clapped. The comedian was moved to tears by
this demonstration of affection from the guests and staff.

Porter Willie Jarvie remembers when Bob Hope came into the
lobby and asked him to phone his wife. 'I got on the hands-free
phone and rang the room number,' says Willie. 'It rang and rang

OPPOSITE:
**ROOM WITH
A VIEW**
*The famous Glendevon
valley viewed from the The
Gleneagles Hotel.*

TRANQUIL SETTING

From their hotel room window, guests look out over spectacular scenery.

and eventually I said, "She's not in her room, Mr Hope." Then I cleared the phone and it immediately began to ring. Presuming it was his wife, Bob Hope picked up the phone and before I had the chance to explain that it was just someone ringing the porter's desk, he said, "Hello . . . Who? Bob Hope here." He put the phone down and said, "That guy's an idiot, he's got the wrong number." I don't know what the poor guest thought, but we were in stitches!'

Bing Crosby was another popular member of Gleneagles 'family'. Ex-General Manager James Bannatyne remembers spotting him in a bank one day when the hotel was holding a pro-celebrity golf tournament. Mr Crosby was cashing about two thousand dollars. He turned to James Bannatyne and said, 'I'm just cashing these dollars – I want some walking about money.' Even today, that would be quite some 'walking about money'! 'Bing Crosby and his family were lovely people,' says Bannatyne. 'On Sundays he would hold family worship in his room. He was a very good man. His two sons were exceptionally well mannered. When you walked around the dinner table in the evening they always stood up for you, and that was nice to see in an era when traditional values were breaking down.'

The lively comic Ronnie Corbett has his own highly unusual Gleneagles memory. He is probably the only person to have self-trephined at the hotel! 'I shut my finger in the car door and gave myself a very painful black nail,' he explains. 'The previous year, when I had managed to do the same thing, my doctor had carried out a process called 'trephining' on me. So I decided to 'self-trephine'. To the horror of the hotel staff, I took a paper clip, undid it except for the last band, leaving an L-shaped end, heated it to red hot then touched my nail with it. The bruised blood shot out, relieving the pain. Spectacular, but not for the squeamish.'

Mr Corbett has enjoyed many happy occasions on the golf course, participating in the pro-celebrity tournaments. Having been brought up in Edinburgh, he is somewhat of a local boy and has early memories of the 'Highland Palace'. 'The Gleneagles Hotel has always had an aura of glamour. I remember as a young boy being aware of this fabulous palace, and being fascinated by the comings and goings of the rich and famous. Now the hotel has reached out to a broader audience. You can pay a green fee and play a round of golf, whereas before you had to be a guest or a member of one of the clubs. Gleneagles has retained its air of mystique while becoming more friendly, which is an enticing combination.'

Tennis star Virginia Wade became the hotel's touring professional in 1983. 'I am a quarter Scottish myself, so have a special feeling for Scotland,' she says. 'Visiting Gleneagles is like going home – you see all your old friends like Billy Lynch and Lt Colonel Ron Smith. Ginger the cat would sit proudly at the front door and John, the lovely doorman, would come out to greet me. Tennis in Scotland is always an experience. You never know if it will rain, snow or just be bitterly cold – and that's in the summer! But I always look forward to returning to Gleneagles.'

Jackie Stewart, three times Formula One Motor Racing Champion, crack clay pigeon shot, and the man who created the Jackie Stewart Shooting School, is also part of the hotel's history. A man of supreme efficiency, Jackie always keeps a trunk at Gleneagles with a range of clothes in it. If he is to attend a function he will phone in advance and let the staff know what he needs. The appropriate clothing will then be taken from his trunk, ironed and laid out ready for him to wear.

GLENEAGLES FAMILIES

Celebrities do not have a monopoly on The Gleneagles Experience. There are many guests, some of whom have been coming for years, and some who are new friends, who feel a special bond with the hotel.

THE McPHERSONS

Dr McPherson, who has been coming to the hotel for over 70 years, remembers being taken to tea at Gleneagles by his parents in 1926. 'My mother lined up my brother and I outside the hotel, and adjusted our ties. She then licked the palm of her hand and made sure our hair was sitting right. "You're entering the world of a famous hotel. Conduct yourselves well," she ordered.'

Dr McPherson and his wife, Muriel, have the honour of being the most senior members of the Gleneagles 'family'. Happily married for 56 years, the McPhersons have become part of the hotel folklore. They take the Glenkinchie Suite in the summer and indulge their passion for golf. In 1973, Dr McPherson, together with another regular guest, Mr Rappaport, initiated the McPherson/Rappaport Golf Trophy for the Gleneagles staff. The tournament has been held every year since then and is an opportunity for two men who have grown to regard Gleneagles as a second home to pay back the staff for their loyal service and unfailing attention. Impressive prizes are on offer to the 90 or so men and women who enter the tournament, and if anyone wins the trophy 3 times in a row, they are given a cruise on one of Mr Rappaport's ships.

THE SHOPPING ARCADE

GETTING AWAY FROM IT ALL and taking things easy in the calm tranquil atmosphere of The Highlands will fulfil many a guest's requirement for a countryside break, but the eager shopper should not despair – a stay at Gleneagles does not spell deprivation. Just a few steps away from Reception guests can discover the joy of choosing beautiful things in the range of shops that compose The Shopping Arcade.

Mappin & Webb's shop was the first to appear at Gleneagles, and was set up before the arcade itself was built. Manageress Christine Horner and Shuna, her able assistant, are waiting to greet you and help you choose beautiful gifts for friends and loved ones.

This Mappin & Webb, a mini version of the bigger stores found all over the UK, is a veritable Aladdin's cave of jewels and gifts. Browse through the goods and try on gorgeous gold necklaces and stunning diamond earrings. The silver photo frames, and range of clocks and watches make fine birthday presents. Very popular is the Herend giftware from Hungary.

Once you've entered into the spirit of spend, spend, spend, you can indulge yourself further by turning right out of Mappin & Webb, and entering The Shopping Arcade of Gleneagles.

In keeping with the tradition of golf, the first shop you see is The Wee Golf Shop. Run by Lynda and May, this is a small version of the bigger shop in the Dormy Clubhouse, and stocks everything the intrepid golfer might require – caps, golf balls, ties, silk scarves, and, vital in this green and fertile land, umbrellas. Children are not forgotten and can buy their own specially designed tiny golf bags. The elegant Gleneagles luggage range is a suitable reminder of your visit.

If you're feeling a little chilly in the Scottish Highlands, then the next shop is just for you. In N Peal you can wrap yourself up in the delicious softness of pure cashmere.

An oasis of warm, beautiful, soft fabrics and colours awaits you. I could have spent all day (and a fortune) in here. Cashmere is very feminine and also very flattering. Brenda Green runs the shop, which receives its stock from the main N Peal shop in London. She has a wide ranging clientele, from local residents to male guests looking for presents for their wives.

Brenda is also in charge of the men's clothing shop, Lords. Now it's the turn of the women to buy their menfolk presents. Here you can find elegant ties, silk handkerchiefs, stylish bow ties and beautiful scarves. Just the thing to transform the man in your life from bedraggled, damp golfer to sophisticated dining companion.

Luxury goods are delicious, tempting, and hardly in short supply in The Shopping Arcade. Yet every guest needs the more mundane necessities too, such as newspapers, books, soap and toothpaste. Exit Lord's, cross the beautiful, polished wood circle and turn the corner into the hotel shop called, appropriately enough, Essentials.

As well as supplying newspapers, magazines, pharmaceutical products, shortbread, maps, guides to Scotland and cigarettes, Essentials also stocks a large selection of gifts.

This year yo-yos are proving the most popular gift, for adults and children alike. They might be the latest fad for teenagers but there have been a few grandmothers who have given impressive demonstrations of how it should be done!

Linda and Lorna keep things moving along between 7.00 am and 7.00 pm, and Sheena and Brenda work part-time.

Take a few steps back from Essentials and you will find yourself inside Burberrys. The shop was opened ten years ago and is managed by Caroline Kummerer. Caroline sells the familiar, classic Burberrys rainwear and leisure wear, as well as delightful teddy bears, perfume, and gifts to suit every member of the family.

A fascinating shop which conjures up images of back streets in Casablanca, with Humphrey Bogart lookalikes lurking in the dark corners of smoky bars and clubs, is Herbert Love.

As soon as you walk in you smell the sweet, rich aroma of high quality cigars. This is manageress Marion's territory. Marion ensures that the shop is kept at a certain humidity, which keeps the cigars in peak condition. There is a large humidor that stores the most expensive cigars, and other humidors stand ready to be purchased by cigar lovers, who come from all corners of the world in pursuit of an excellent smoke.

As the shop stocks some of the best Cuban cigars, it is very popular with

Americans, who are still prohibited from purchasing the famous Cuban cigars in their own country.

Marion has noticed that not all her customers are male. 'Cigars are becoming very popular with women, and that is opening up a whole new market for us,' she says.

If you thought Harvey Nicks was only to be found in London or Leeds, then you are wrong. A small, perfectly formed miniature of the big store is right here at Gleneagles. Run by the elegant Isobel Donaldson, it stocks a little bit of everything – richly coloured devoré scarves, handbags, jeans, T-shirts, jewellery, socks, hair accessories and gentlemen's shirts and ties. Visitors to Isobel's shop form a real Harvey Nichols fan club, and aficionados will travel from far and wide for the chance to visit a miniature version of the world-famous Knightsbridge store.

'We do a lot of trade in perfumery, particularly amongst men who are searching for that special gift for their wives or girlfriends,' says Isobel. 'We also have a large number of Club members as customers, and people who make the journey from Perth.'

Another elegant shop in The Shopping Arcade is Mondi, just along from Harvey Nichols. Jane Petrie runs the shop, which stocks stylish and classic day and evening clothes.

Mondi is an extremely popular stopping point for Club members and guests searching for a smart new outfit for dinner or for a party. If you need that last-minute special something, there's a good chance Mondi will be able to oblige.

REGULAR GUESTS
Dr and Mrs McPherson (right) with Mr and Mrs Rappaport celebrate the 20th anniversary of the McPherson/Rappaport Golf Trophy organised for the staff.

Dr McPherson's 80th birthday provided the reason for a great celebration. The staff held a party and presented him with a painting of The King's Course. Golf is in the McPherson's blood – they are godparents to Gary Player's youngest daughter, and stay with Jack Nicklaus and his family when they visit the US. Dr McPherson is the first honorary member of the Gleneagles Golf Club, and Mrs McPherson is the second, followed by Jackie Stewart, Jack Nicklaus, Sean Connery and HRH The Duke of York. As Dr McPherson says, 'Gleneagles is all about people. The staff are outstanding and make you feel like one of the family.'

When Dr McPherson found an old bill which charged him £39.50 a day for the Glenkinchie Suite (which is the same suite he has stayed in ever since), the management proved they could take a joke. Dr McPherson sent a letter to the hotel, in which he wrote: 'My wife and I are contemplating a holiday and your hotel comes highly recommended. We would appreciate the same rates as previously charged.' When the final bill came, they discovered they'd been charged £39.50 for the entire stay. Being a upstanding man, Dr McPherson wrote to say he couldn't possibly accept this, to which the manager replied, 'In view of the integrity you have shown, you can have the first night on the hotel and the second on me.' Dr McPherson is now frantically searching for a 1926 bill , when dinner cost 7 shillings and sixpence!

THE LEWISES

Mr and Mrs Lewis have celebrated several important events at Gleneagles and in 1995 honoured their silver wedding there with champagne and a strawberry tea. In 1997 they returned for a fortnight to commemorate Mrs Lewis's 50th birthday.

In 1998 their son William found himself having to make a major decision. He was studying at the University of Ealing in London and working part-time at Harrods. Harrods offered him a rare place on its prestigious and highly selective management training course. Having worked flat out for three months, William needed to take a break and sit down with his parents to discuss his future. The Lewis family decided that the soothing, nurturing atmosphere of Gleneagles would be the perfect location in which to help everyone think lucidly and allow William the space to make an important decision. They were right. William decided to accept the offer and now is well on the way to a top career with the luxury store.

Gleneagles also serves as a true healing sanctuary for Mrs Lewis, who suffers a serious heart condition. 'Because of my health, I have to be very careful about what I do,' she says. 'I need a room with no sun, where I can take things slowly and won't be disturbed before 2.00 pm. The Gleneagles personnel go out of their way to make sure I'm looked after and happy. I like blues and pinks and they always put us in a room with blue and pink decor, which is also quiet and cool. The staff here are always incredibly thoughtful. No request is ever too much trouble.'

If things do go wrong, the staff quickly put it right. In 1995, Mrs Lewis wanted to book a visit for the Easter period. She telephoned and requested a brochure. Ten days went by and she heard nothing. She called a second and a third time, but again, silence. Finally, she made a brief, abrupt call to the hotel. When the family arrived they found they had been upgraded, at no extra cost, to a suite with two bedrooms, two bathrooms and fourteen windows. That's saying sorry with style!

The Lewises have stayed in some of the world's best hotels – Reid's in Madeira, the George V in Paris, The Dorchester in London – yet Gleneagles remains untouchable. 'It's the little personal touches. Whenever we have something to celebrate, or a major decision to make, we know exactly where to come.'

THE WESTGATES

The Westgates are also well-established members of the Gleneagles extended family. They have been coming to the hotel since the mid-1980s, when they decided to take their three children to Scotland, as an alternative to their customary holiday destination of the south of France. It was love at first sight. 'When we arrived at Gleneagles we were most impressed with the hotel,' remembers Mrs Westgate. 'There was such a range of activities on offer. The Shooting School had just been opened and we all became very friendly with Justin Jones [who ran the school] and his family. My husband and two sons are keen golfers, and they would disappear off to The King's Course while my daughter and I amused ourselves on the Wee Course. We love the Dormy Clubhouse and all the characters that are associated with golf at Gleneagles. Tom Watson, who is the starter on The King's Course, is a real star, with an endless supply of golfing tales up his sleeve.

'Whenever we visit, Billy Lynch says, "Welcome home." And that's exactly how we feel – as though we are staying in our own Scottish home from home.'

Gleneagles is a real haven for Mr Westgate, its range of leisure activities providing him with the chance to unwind from a high-powered job and really relax. As his wife says, 'We manage to completely switch off at Gleneagles. Everything seems a million miles away. My husband can forget about work and even forget what day of the week it is. We always have breakfast on room service. One day I did appear in the dining room for breakfast and the staff were so shocked to see me they rolled out the red carpet! We have made so many friends there – Marketing Manager Terry Waldron often comes to visit us.

'We spend Christmas at Gleneagles with Justin and Emma Jones and another regular Gleneagles family, the Longbottoms. When our three families get together in The Strathearn Restaurant on Christmas Day, it's a riot. One Christmas my daughter suddenly said, "Look, Mummy, the trolley's on fire," and sure enough, there was a dinner trolley blazing away beside us as we were happily tucking into our Christmas lunch. Before we knew it there were firemen rushing through the restaurant. It was hilarious, and didn't spoil the day at all.'

THE CRAWFORDS

Newer members of the Gleneagles family are the Crawfords, who come from Ireland and visit the hotel regularly with their nine-year-old twin daughters. Dr Robert Crawford first came to enjoy the golf, but it was with some trepidation. He felt that a hotel that was used to the patronage of royalty and celebrities might be stuffy and snooty, and have little time for the discerning, normal person looking for a short break. As he quickly discovered, his fears were unfounded. 'I felt relaxed from the moment I arrived. The hotel strikes a great balance between informality and high quality. By the second day the staff were greeting me by name.'

With two children to keep happy, Dr Crawford and his wife, Hilary, need a range of diversions at hand, and Gleneagles certainly provides it. The kids love the outdoor 'hot pool', which they can sit in even when there's snow and ice on the ground, and Dr and Mrs Crawford love the 'lap pool', where they can get in some serious swimming. Then Mrs Crawford can indulge in a little discreet shopping while her husband battles with force 5 gales on the golf course. An 18 handicap, Dr Crawford believes The King's Course is the most challenging, The Queen's Course the tightest and The Monarch's Course the one with the easiest and widest fairway.

Birthdays in the Gleneagles family are celebrated in style – the Crawford twins' birthday falls, appropriately, on the Glorious 12th. In 1998, the twins had a birthday they will never forget.

Ian Ironside, creator of the hotel's famous 'marzipan men', made cakes for the girls, which were a great success. 'When we took the girls to thank Ian,' says Mrs Crawford, 'he presented them each with a marzipan animal – a cat and a dog – which they installed in pride of place on the windowsill in our room. It was an occasion they'll remember for the rest of their lives.'

COLIN FREEDMAN

Colin Freedman has been a Gleneagles guest since the early 1970s, initially as part of a group of executives from the pharmaceutical giant, Bayer. He feels the Gleneagles magic comes from its completeness. 'The quality is everywhere,' he says. When I invite people here they never cancel. It's expensive, but perceived as being very good value. And there's that priceless feeling of being pampered.

'Peter Lederer has given the hotel a facelift and the facilities are now superb. The Club is fantastic, and The Shopping Arcade excellent. No-one cares about the weather – we're all having too much of a good time. I remember one time I was playing golf with some friends and there was a clap of thunder. The caddies raced off the course, but we were eager to play on. Unfortunately, we had no golf clubs. The only time I've seen the caddies move like that is when they spot the tax man!'

Colin Freedman remembers one particular time when he complained about the lack of haggis on the menu. When he was next in The Strathearn, the lights were suddenly dimmed and a huge tray was brought out with a large haggis on it, lit up by a candle. When he looked up, Mr Freedman caught sight of Executive Head Chef Mike Picken peeping round the door with a big grin on his face!

LIFE IN THE DINING ROOM

The Westgates love dining in The Strathearn. 'Ahmet Yurdakol, the maitre d'hotel, is delightful,' says Mrs Westgate. 'As soon as he sees us, he's ready with the drinks. We adore crêpe suzette and Ahmet loves arranging for it to be made especially for us. He'll do anything for us and we appreciate that.'

Ahmet Yurdakol has been at Gleneagles for 28 years and is still in love with the place. He can't see himself returning to his native Turkey. 'I went back in the summer with my son,' he says, 'but it was too hot.' He lives in Auchterarder with his English wife and is happy working at Gleneagles, the place he fell in love with nearly thirty years go. Ahmet's work is vital in making sure the guests are kept happy. 'The first thing I do when I arrive for work is check which VIPs are attending, and see whether we have any of our regular guests, who might prefer a certain table. I love my job because I love people and because something new happens every day.'

If the restaurant is full, then there are over 200 people to seat at once and 30 waiters attending to their needs. A full restaurant puts intense pressure on the kitchen staff, who have to second guess what people are likely to order. Waiters are trained to sell the specialities of the day, like the roast, but there are always some people who will want their own favourites. The latest computer technology has eased the pressure somewhat – now all orders go straight into the computer system to be processed, along with any important information such as which foods need re-ordering – but catering for a full restaurant will always be a major organisational feat that demands a great deal of effort and concentration from every member of staff involved.

ENSURING QUALITY SERVICE
Ahmet Yurdakol (left), the maitre d'hotel, with Elaine Watson, the Restaurant Manager, and Vicente Herras, the Assistant Restaurant Manager.

Steamed Roast Duck

WITH PEAR

1 tsp salt

½ tsp cajun spices

1 duck crown or 2 large duck breasts

2.5 cm/1 inch piece of fresh ginger

1 carrot, peeled and roughly chopped

1 onion, peeled and roughly chopped

sprig of thyme & rosemary

600 ml/1 pint water

½ orange, ½ lemon

a little vegetable oil

For the pancake

½ egg

30 ml/1 fl oz milk

30 g/1½ oz plain flour

75 g/3 oz cooked barley

½ tsp baking powder

1 tsp chopped parsley

60 g/2½ oz mashed potato

salt and pepper to taste

For the garnish

1 pear, peeled, cored and halved

2 spring onions, chopped

1 tsp thinly shredded pickled ginger

a little olive oil

½ red, ½ green, ½ yellow pepper, sliced

2 sprigs fresh tarragon, shredded

For the sauce

1 small shallot, finely chopped

a knob of butter

60 ml/2 fl oz port

250 ml/7 fl oz game or duck stock

You need to start this dish the day before you cook it. Your butcher can prepare a duck crown for you, which is simply the duck with the legs cut off. Steaming the duck opens the pores in the fat and as a result when pan frying you have a crisper duck skin.

RUB THE SALT and cajun spices into the duck crown or breasts. Leave overnight for the salt to be absorbed into the crown.

Chop the unpeeled ginger. Place the chopped carrot, onion, herbs and ginger into a large saucepan with the water. Add the orange and lemon and bring to the boil. Meanwhile, heat a little vegetable oil in a heavy-based pan and sear the duck crown or breasts until lightly browned all over. Place a colander on top of the saucepan as an insert to hold the duck in place. Put the duck into the colander and cover with a lid.

If using the duck crown, steam for approximately 15 minutes; steam the breasts for 7–8 minutes. The duck will be cooked halfway through. Remove from the colander and, if using the crown, remove the breasts. (The crown carcass can be used for stock.) Put the breasts to one side.

Make a pancake by beating the egg and milk together, folding in the flour and adding the barley, baking powder and parsley. Add the mashed potatoes and season to taste. You are looking to achieve a firm mixture that falls off the spoon. Divide the mixture into two pancake shapes. Heat a little vegetable oil in a small pan. Cook each pancake in the pan, or use a

6 cm/2 inch mould in a larger pan, on a medium heat, for approximately 2 minutes on each side, until golden brown. Keep the pancakes warm.

For the garnish, cut the pears from top to bottom into 2.5 cm/1 inch thick slices. Mix with the pickled ginger, chopped spring onions, green, yellow and red peppers, and the tarragon. Flash fry in olive oil and season to taste. Keep warm.

For the sauce, sauté the shallot in the butter until translucent then add the port. Reduce by one-third then add the game or duck stock. Reduce by a further three quarters and pass through a fine sieve or tea strainer. Taste the sauce and adjust the seasoning. Keep warm.

Preheat the oven to 190°C/375°F/gas mark 5. Place the duck breasts back into a hot frying pan, skin side down, to crisp up the skin, then place onto a baking tray and finish in the oven for 5 minutes.

To serve, place some warm garnish on each plate and place a warm pancake alongside. Slice each duck breast and arrange on top of the garnish. Pour a little sauce around on each plate.

Serves 2

Good accompaniment:
A red Châteauneuf-du-Pape from the Rhône

MIKE PICKEN – EXECUTIVE HEAD CHEF

*T*HE EXECUTIVE HEAD CHEF has overall responsibility for the kitchens. Under him is a senior sous chef, three other sous chefs, a chef de partie for each section (sauces, fish, vegetables, meat etc), the 1st commis chef, the 2nd commis chef and the trainees and work experience staff.

Unlike other celebrity chefs, Mike Picken is not prone to tantrums or prima donna complexes. He is calm, quiet and authoritative – just the man for running a large hotel which has 4 general outlets, and 13 outlets for functions. In a job where your own personality comes second, a Marco Pierre White or a Gordon Ramsay would simply not fit in.

Mike hails from Torquay, and at 16 went to catering college to pursue his interest in cookery. After a trip to Australia with his wife to be, he came to Gleneagles as a chef de partie in 1990 to realise his ambition of working with Alan Hill. Mike soon graduated through the positions of sous chef and senior sous chef, before taking over the top job when Alan moved to his post of food and beverage manager.

Every Wednesday, the Events department sends Mike information on all the new bookings and functions. He classifies it according to the relevant food sections, then defines the various responsibilities. The sous chefs get together and highlight special requests – a guest may ask for one of Ian Ironside's ice carvings, or require a meal prepared according to a particular theme. If the special request is repeat

business, then Mike makes sure his staff check to see what the guests had before, and what their likes and dislikes are. However, even at Gleneagles there are times when things do go wrong.

One such occasion was an outside function at Blair Atholl Castle. The kitchen staff had worked hard to prepare for the event, and by 9.00 pm on the previous evening a van had been loaded with everything required for the following day's function, except the food.

All the preparations were going swimmingly until someone picked up a menu and by chance discovered that the dessert they'd just prepared was not the same as the one on the menu. Two hundred and twenty desserts had to be made overnight.

Mike is now involved in a lot of overseas promotional trips, where he represents Gleneagles' culinary expertise to potential or existing markets. Taking The Gleneagles

Experience to the rest of the world is an exciting, if demanding exercise. Mike always allows plenty of time. This extra time was essential on a recent trip to Thailand, where he ended up with 200 grouse – at the wrong airport.

Managing Director Peter Lederer admires Mike's ability to look for something different. 'Mike will always try out something new, and is never scared of it not working out. To be at the leading edge of food development we need to have an Executive Head Chef like Mike, who will bring new and exciting things to Gleneagles.'

When not at the hotel, Mike still tends to be found in the kitchen. 'I enjoy cooking at home. I'm quite likely to be found making pancakes with my kids on Sunday morning and messing about in the kitchen with them. It is a great way to relax from the pressures of work, even if I am doing the same job.'

88

CONSTANT
CHANGE
*Once breakfast is over The
Strathearn Restaurant
must be cleaned and made
ready for the evening, then
again for the following day.*

One thing that has changed in The Strathearn Restaurant over the years is the dress code. On Friday and Saturday evenings people used to wear black tie, now it is smart or casual attire – a change that has not met with unanimous approval from the guests. Ahmet has seen many celebrities pass through the doors of The Strathearn – Bob Hope had his birthday here, and Jack Lemmon, Bruce Forsyth, George C Scott and Sean Connery have all feasted in the beautiful dining room. The dining tables are clad in fine linen tablecloths, with crystal glasses, silver-plated cutlery which has a design based on the original 1924 design, and Dudson Fine China plates.

AT THE FOREFRONT OF FOOD

Gleneagles has to ensure it remains at the cutting edge of food development. The men responsible for observing trends and responding to changes in taste and eating habits are Alan Hill, the Food and Beverage Manager, and Mike Picken, the Executive Head Chef.

Gleneagles has built up a team of loyal outside suppliers. One such supplier is Simon Howie of Simon Howie Butchers of Auchterarder. The Gleneagles Hotel is about high-quality food, served fresh and exquisitely cooked, and Simon Howie is the man who caters for all the hotel's meat needs – terrines, fillet steak with *foie gras*, sirloin steaks trimmed to exact specifications, mousses and game.

Simon has built up a successful business that now includes four retail outlets and a state-of-the-art meat factory, which is based in Dunning. As the industry's needs have changed, Simon's business has adapted to provide a specialised service. The success of The Gleneagles Hotel has enabled businesses in the community to

THE ROAST
TROLLEY
*The roast is carved at table
to the diner's requirement.*

Cutlet and Loin of Lamb

WITH PARSNIP AND APPLE COMPOTE

For the parsnip and apple compote

1 large parsnip

1 large apple

50 g/2 oz butter

1 large shallot, diced

For the garnish

1 baking potato

100 g/4 oz fine green beans

50 g/2 oz shallots, cut into fine rings

50 g/2 oz red pepper, finely diced

100 g/4 oz borlotti beans, cooked

For the lamb and sauce

a little vegetable oil

400 g/14 oz single loin of lamb (trimmed to leave a little fat)

4 lamb cutlets

50 ml/1¾ fl oz red wine

50 ml/1¾ fl oz balsamic vinegar

600 ml/1 pint lamb stock

salt and freshly ground black pepper

For the apple chip

1 apple, cored but unpeeled

icing sugar

90

This dish was created for a competition where it won a gold medal. Its popularity with guests and staff alike has established it as a signature dish.

❖

PEEL AND DICE the parsnip and blanch for 10 minutes in boiling salted water. Peel and core the apple and cut into dice. Heat 15 g/¼ oz of the butter in a heavy-based frying pan and cook the shallot just until translucent. Add the parsnips and apple and a little seasoning. Cook slowly over a slow flame until the compote breaks down. Keep the compote warm.

Cut or turn the potato into 8 long, thin barrel shapes approximately 3 cm/1½ inches long. Pan-fry the potato in the remaining butter until golden brown and cooked through. Cut the green beans into fine diamonds and blanch in boiling water. Drain well. Mix with the shallot rings, finely diced red pepper and cooked borlotti beans. Set aside.

Preheat the oven to 200°C/400°F/gas mark 6. Heat a little vegetable oil in a heavy-based frying pan and sear the loin all over. Place in the oven for 5-6 minutes for pink lamb, or a little longer if you prefer it more well done. Fry the cutlets in the pan for 2 minutes for rare, 3 minutes for medium and 9 minutes for well done.

Tip out any excess fat and deglaze the pan with the red wine, vinegar and the meat stock. Reduce the mixture until a sauce consistency is reached. Correct the seasoning and sieve the sauce.

To assemble the dish, place a quarter of the compote in the middle of each plate and lay a cutlet on top with the bone pointing up. Slice the loin into 12 and place 3 slices on top of each compote. Heat the garnish gently in a pan and scatter around each plate. Place two of the potato barrels into the compote, pointing up. Spoon the sauce around and serve.

The addition of an apple chip makes the dish even more spectacular.

Slice the apple horizontally into 1 mm/⅛ inch thick slices. Dip in the icing sugar and place the slices on a non-stick, oiled tray. Cook in a slow oven until lightly coloured.

Serves 4

Good accompaniment:
A good burgundy such as Gevry Chambertin

flourish and expand, and nowhere is this more ably demonstrated than at Simon Howie's premises.

Simon says, 'We provide Gleneagles with a very comprehensive service. They buy steaks from us, as opposed to whole sirloins. We trim the steaks to the Gleneagles specification and supply exactly what they are looking for. We know the history of our meat, and have a rigid control of our suppliers. Because we are local we can provide a very personalised service, so we supply the hotel seven days a week and visit two or three times a day, or more if needed.'

Scottish produce is prepared under the strictest of hygiene and food safety conditions. With craft butchery, product innovation, and unrivalled standards of service, Simon Howie Butchers is a prime example of a successful business that has grown on the back of Gleneagles. As an entrepreneur, Simon spotted the opportunity offered by the hotel's presence, and makes sure that the customer gets the best quality for the best value. Gleneagles has a policy of supporting local businesses and bringing jobs to the surrounding area and Simon knows how much his growing business owes Gleneagles.

'We provide the butchery expertise, but it is thanks to Gleneagles that we have been able to grow and develop into a large, thriving business. We are constantly looking at ways in which we can develop further, and provide Gleneagles' guests with new, exciting products of optimum quality.'

92

PASTRY AND BREAD

Afternoon tea is one of the highlights of a Sunday afternoon in the Highlands, and Gleneagles is the people's choice for a sumptuous tea served in The Bar.

Darran Ridley is the Head Pastry Chef. Often there are 12 different cakes to choose from for tea, plus the delicate sandwiches and shortbread and biscuits that are made to the carefully controlled Gleneagles recipes.

Master cake and pastry maker Ian Ironside is responsible for the famous Gleneagles 'marzipan men'. He is also the creator of the many impressive wedding cakes and other celebration cakes, and the wonderful display carvings in fat, sugar and ice that grace the banquets. If a company wants to have its logo on its cake or pastry, then Ian will create a stunning design in fat, sugar, ice or chocolate. For the McDonalds' Women's Open Golf Championship, for example, he made 150 little Ronald McDonalds as gifts for the customers.

Ian has spent a lifetime as a pastry chef, and first came to Gleneagles in 1958. He has won top awards, such as the gold medal at Olympia for sugar, bread and confectionery. He is also a Member

DARRAN RIDLEY

ALAN HILL – FOOD & BEVERAGE MANAGER

*A*LAN HILL joined Gleneagles in 1989, when the hotel was just emerging from a rough patch. Alan explains the scenario: 'Everything in the restaurant was very clinical and the skill base had been run down. We had young, enthusiastic people, but their skills were not being channelled. We wanted to encourage people to perform at a level beyond which they believed themselves capable. It's only natural for people to suffer a certain amount of self-doubt – the important thing is to move beyond that. We wanted to increase the quality of the food and drink, and also increase profitability. It was important for the staff to understand what they were working towards. Until a few years ago, Elaine Watson, the Restaurant Manager, had not actually eaten the food she was offering to the guests. Now we encourage our managers to try out what they are giving to the guests, so they can understand more about the food we offer.'

Over the last five years or so, the desire to know more about the food we eat has increased considerably. Guests are more educated about food and drink, more discerning and more well travelled. Alan has already bought the millennium champagne – the entire

UK stock of Dom Perignon 1985 and 6 jeroboams of Dom Perignon 1993, which are maturing in Dom Perignon's original cellars. In addition, the hotel has 204 magnums of Moët 1990, 4818 bottles of Moët 1992, and 54 magnums of Moët 1992. So there's not too much chance of running dry during the celebrations for the Gleneagles millennium!

Alan has developed a strategy for each of his outlets, The Strathearn Restaurant, The Bar, The Club, The Dormy Clubhouse and Room Service.

The Strathearn offers a world class, classic dining experience, with the highest quality Scottish cuisine. It recreates a sophisticated 1920s feel, in a spacious, high-ceilinged dining room.

The Bar is more relaxed, offering classic cocktails, fresh coffee, traditional teas and snacks and a massive selection of whiskies, cognacs, wines and beers, while The Club offers a more international feel, serving American, Italian and Mediterranean cuisine in a fun, family environment. Golfers and their families are catered for in the Dormy Clubhouse, which has a traditional, pub-like atmosphere, and serves home-made pies, grills and many different beers and ales.

Alan knows only too well the importance of the people factor. 'The social skills of our staff are really first class,' he says. 'I believe we are true masters of the ancient art of Scottish hospitality.'

93

of Master Bakers, a Member of the *Académie Culinaire de France*, and a Fellow of the Academy of Culinary Arts. He recalls one particular Saturday night early on in his Gleneagles career when the restaurant ran out of fruit, and he was sent to get some more supplies.

'I put a load of fruit into my apron and dashed off to replace the empty fruit bowls,' says Ian. 'Unfortunately, I ran straight into the Head Chef, and nearly

IAN IRONSIDE

94

pushed him over. "Boy, walk, don't run," he said.' In those days, the Head Chef ruled his kitchen with a rod of iron – you either did what you were told or, if you couldn't take the heat, then you got out of the kitchen. It was a tough training, and you learnt fast. In fact, running around collecting fruit was already an improvement on Ian's first job at the hotel, which was to gut and pluck 24 wild duck!

Before specialising in pastry, Ian was expected to work in all areas of the kitchen. In those days, discipline was as rigid for the guests as it was for the staff. When a gentleman guest appeared in his slippers at Reception one morning to complain that he hadn't received his morning paper, he was requested to put on proper shoes.

As Head Pastry Chef (before Darran Ridley took over this role), Ian would spend all morning preparing afternoon teas, then prepare the ice creams, before returning at 5.00 pm to start on the petits fours for the evening meal. The petits fours were intricate creations which would take him a good hour to prepare. They included grapes in sugar, macaroons, *langues de chats*, gooseberries in sugar, strawberries in fondant, Turkish delight and chocolate and caramel sweets.

Of course Ian would also have to prepare the pastry for Fillet of Beef Wellington and for the Salmon en Croûte. Then there was the choux pastry for the eclairs, cheese straws for the soup, and small pastry cases for the vol-au-vents. The pace was relentless, but the staff never forgot how to look after each other. 'The lady in charge of dispensing the wine was a Mrs Williams. She loved ice cream so the Head Chef would make sure he took her an ice cream every night,' says Ian.

Ian has devoted his entire career to creating spectacular displays and making celebration cakes and gifts. Gleneagles has been his life. 'It's a first-class training ground for youngsters, and a great environment in which to let your imagination run wild and create displays that will make a corporate event that little bit more special,' he says. Ian has seen the technology change quite a bit too: 'We used to use a chisel for the ice displays, but now all modern carvers use a power saw,' he explains. 'It makes it much quicker, although I prefer traditional methods.'

Dave Hill is the bread man, working alongside Ian in the kitchen. His morning starts at 4.00 am, when he arrives to prepare the bread for breakfast. The standard loaves are fruit, brown, brioche, French stick, walnut, wholemeal, rye and granary. At dinner, guests choose between three types of bread roll – plain white, herb and onion (which can be changed for other varieties), or cheese.

Dave's objective is to listen to what the guests want and to perfect the varieties of breads on offer. 'In the future I want to develop the specialised breads. The guests now travel widely and have sampled many different breads from all over the world. They get to know which types they like and it is my job to make sure we are keeping up with the latest tastes and novelties,' he says.

MARRYING FOOD AND WINE

Good food and good wine are an essential part of The Gleneagles Experience, and the man in charge of wines is Head Wine Waiter Paul Hinton. Paul works together with Head Waiter Angus MacMillan to make sure that all the guests have the drink they want. Their in-depth knowledge of wine means a connoisseur can select the best wines available, such as the Château Petrus 1970 or the Château Margaux 1961, another excellent vintage wine.

Each restaurant has its own exclusive wine list, so if you select a wine in The Strathearn, you can be sure it will not be duplicated in any of the other restaurants at Gleneagles.

Not everyone can afford a highly expensive bottle of wine, nor do they always want one, and both Angus and Paul pride themselves as much on choosing a good house wine as they do on recognising some of the best wines in the world. As Angus says, 'We have about seven or eight suppliers, and they give us a very good service. We have over 14,000 bottles of wine in the wine cellar, and there are 172 bins available on the main wine list. But if someone asks for a particular wine that isn't on the list, we can get it very quickly for them. We're often called to give advice on tourist spots and leisure activities as well. We need to be knowledgeable on a range of subjects.

'We make sure we're very well informed about vintages, and we are always given plenty of warning when a particular vintage is about to run out. It is equally important to be able to advise the guests on the best time to drink the different red and white wines,' says Angus. 'Red wine has a high tannin and low fruit content, and as it matures the tannin levels fall and the fruit blooms,' he explains. 'When the levels are about equal the wine has peaked, and a peaked wine will have a very rounded taste. You can see the colour change – as it matures it becomes lighter around the edges.'

Wine choice can be defined by nationality. The Brits and Irish will go for traditional red wines, like claret, which is the English term for Bordeaux reds. Port is also very popular with the English. The Japanese go for standard whites like Chablis, and old-fashioned French reds, while the Americans adore Chardonnay. Chablis is made from the chardonnay grape, but people often refuse a Chablis, because they are unaware of this.

Angus matches the wine to the guest, and also to the food the guest is going to eat. 'You can generally judge the type of wine the guest will like by the way he or she is dressed. 'We like to have a laugh with the guests. We had one lovely eccentric gentleman in the restaurant, and when he asked for a port we said, "A Dover or a Folkestone?" He loved the joke.'

Matching food to wine is very important, as is drinking the right water – a still mineral water is a much

WINE EXPERTS
Angus MacMillan and Paul Hinton ensure the guests have a wide selection of quality wines to accompany their food.

Scallops

WITH FENNEL, PEPPER AND ARTICHOKES

1 stalk lemon grass

8 extra large scallops with coral

75 g/3 oz butter

1 small shallot, chopped

1 bay leaf

2 peppercorns

150 ml/¼ pint white wine

100 ml/3¾ fl oz chicken stock

100 ml/3¾ fl oz double cream

1 fennel

selection of fresh herbs

2 tinned artichokes

1 small red pepper

a little olive oil

100 ml/3¾ fl oz basil oil

salt and milled pepper to taste

For the basil oil

600 ml/1 pint olive oil

1 packet basil

The best scallops to use are the extra large king scallops. The basil oil needs to be made at least 24 hours in advance.

STRIP THE LEMON GRASS lengthways until you find the hard middle core. Cut this into quarters lengthways and use it to skewer 2 scallops together. Repeat with the other 6 scallops.

To make the sauce, finely shred the outer covering of the lemon grass. Melt 25 g/1 oz of the butter in a heavy-based pan, add the lemon grass, shallots, bay leaf and peppercorns and cook uncovered until translucent. Add 100 ml/3 fl oz of the white wine and reduce by two-thirds. Add the chicken stock and reduce by the same amount again. Finally, add the double cream and reduce to give a light coating consistency. Strain the sauce and correct the seasoning.

To prepare the garnish, trim any blemished outer leaves from the fennel and sauté in the remaining butter to lightly colour it. Preheat the oven to 190°C/375°F/ gas mark 5. Make a tin foil bag, add the fennel, a selection of fresh herbs and the remaining white wine and ensure all the edges are sealed. Place in the oven for approximately 45 minutes, until the fennel feels soft in the centre when pierced with a knife. Allow to cool, then cut into 8 equal-sized pieces, using the root to ensure it does not fall apart. This can be done in advance.

Cut the two artichokes into eighths.

Remove the seeds from the pepper and cut into thin strips approximately 2.5 cm/1 inch long.

If necessary, heat a little olive oil in a heavy-based pan and fry the fennel for 2 minutes or until warmed through. Cook the pepper strips and artichokes in the pan for 2-3 minutes. Season with salt and pepper. Season the scallops and sear on both sides in a very hot non-stick pan or ribbed cooking plate until just cooked in the middle. (They should feel soft to the touch and the middle slightly warmed.)

To assemble the dish, place two pieces of fennel, with a quarter of the artichokes and peppers in the middle of each plate. Place the scallops, still on the skewer, on top. Pour a little lemon grass sauce around the plate. Finally, split the sauce with some basil oil (see below).

To make the basil oil, purée the oil and basil in a blender. Pass the mixture through a fine strainer or muslin into a tall container. Leave to rest to allow the sediment to sink to the bottom. Leave for 24 hours before decanting. You will be left with a clear green basil-scented oil.

Serves 4

Good accompaniment:
Talisker malt whisky, 10 years old, or a white Burgundy – Puligny-Montrachet

better accompaniment to a glass of wine than a sparkling mineral water. A nice white burgundy, like a Meursault 1994 or 1995, goes very well with rich, creamy fish dishes and some poultry. A l'Hermitage red Bordeaux will go well with peppered Angus steak, as it is a very full-bodied spicy, peppery, rich wine, with a flavour of fruits of the forest. A Sauvignon Blanc will go well with game, such as venison and grouse, which are often cooked with herbs and in a gooseberry sauce. Grouse with woodland berries calls for a Rioja, while a traditional Dover Sole will be perfectly matched by a Premier Cru Chablis, a Pouilly-Fumé or a Sancerre, which is a crisp, dry, white wine. Beaujolais Nouveau is excellent with creamy cheeses like camembert and brie. A more pungent cheese calls for a full-bodied red or a port.

There are, of course, a range of dessert wines to accompany your calorie-filled sweets. A Sauternes, for example, is a good accompaniment to white chocolate mousse. Dessert wines have a high sugar content, as the grapes are picked after they are ripe, when there is fungus on them and the sugar levels are high. The fungus is washed off when fermentation is complete, and the result is a sweet white wine.

If you fancy a little champagne, then Angus and Paul have a wide range for you to choose from, from non-vintage Moët, ideal with a lemon sherbet which brings out the fizziness, to the top vintages such as a 1985 Dom Perignon, or a Louis Roederer 1988.

The production of high-quality champagne is dependent upon the skill of the people who turn the bottle in the cellars. They are usually the highest earners in a champagne house, as their skill is based on knowing when and how much to turn the bottle, when to put the sediment in the neck, and when to tell the owner the bottle is ready. There's very little that Angus does not know about champagne: 'An interesting by-product of champagne is a kind of black penicillin which grows on the cellar walls,' he explains. 'If you rub it on a cut, the cut will heal.'

The wine cellars are stacked high with wines from every wine-producing country and region in the world. 'The New World wines are growing in popularity. People are more interested in wine from Australia, New Zealand, South Africa, South America and North America than they were a few years ago. 'In general, Australia's best white wine is Chardonnay and its best reds are Cabernet Sauvignon and Shiraz. New Zealand's best white is Sauvignon Blanc and its best red is Pinot Noir.'

Fancy a magnum of wine to celebrate with your guests? Then try the Château Mouton Rothschild 1981 – good value at £750 a magnum, or £500 a bottle. Or, if you prefer, try a magnum of non-vintage Pommery or Moët. If excess is not your thing, then choose from a range of 27 wines available by the half bottle.

The liqueur trolley is simply laden with temptations. A Louis XIII cognac, an *eau de vie*, an XO Brandy, Courvoisier Hennessy, Rémy Martin, a Sassicaia Grappa and a rather special Da Silva Port. Guests can select a Romeo and Juliet cigar, or any of the many malts on offer.

It helps that both Angus and Paul love their jobs. The service they offer is based on a curiosity about their area of expertise and a real interest in what the guests want, and that is what Gleneagles is all about.

MAGNUS AND THE MALT

Think of Scotland and one of the first things that comes to mind is the divine, mysterious taste of malt whisky – the 'tears of the gods'. Scotland, with its unique weather and pure atmosphere, produces a nectar that warms the heart and soul in the deep midwinter and lifts the spirit in the dull, grey dampness of many a Highland summer.

Malt whisky is known throughout the world, but there are very few people who could be classified as experts. The ultimate whisky expert at Gleneagles is Barman Magnus Heron. Magnus does not follow the traditional image of a malt lover as an old, bearded gentlemen closeted away far from civilisation. He is young, dynamic, very bright, but very much a malt lover.

Magnus's love of whisky began with a summer job at Gleneagles four years ago. 'I helped out in the main dining room as a wine waiter, and then I was offered a full-time job in the lounge, which used to be the drawing room, and then in The Bar. I'd been brought up in a family of malt whisky lovers, and so the nectar was already in my blood. When I started working at Gleneagles I became more and more interested. I began reading about malt whisky, and brought more malts up from the cellars. I created a display, and got talking to the guests about malt.'

There are many processes to go through before a malt is ready for drinking. As with fine wines, one of the most delicate of these is maturation. Maturation is believed to account for between 60 and 80 per cent of the flavour in malt whisky. During evaporation, up to 50 per cent of the flavour, known rather romantically as the 'angel share', can be lost.

At the distillery, the newly made spirit is poured into second-hand casks, which have usually held either bourbon or sherry. This is because the sherry or bourbon seasons the wood and alters its chemical structure in ways that are beneficial to whisky. The cask increases complexity, enhances fragrance and delicacy, creates astringency, lends colour and integrates the other flavours present in the whisky. Not surprisingly, there is lively competition between the distillery companies for the most sought after casks. The casks are used three times.

The length of time the whisky spends in the individual casks is dictated by the particular whisky in question and which type of cask is used.

Unlike wine, whisky does not continue to mature in the bottle, although it will change. Lighter alcohols may find their way through the stoppers in time. Generally speaking, lighter whiskies will mature more quickly than heavier malts. The lighter whiskies are to be found in the lowlands and Speyside. Magnus and his colleagues have developed the famous Gleneagles Six – a collection of six classic malts which are perfect for a guests' tasting session.

MAGNUS HERON

GETTING TO KNOW THE GOLDEN NECTAR

In 1998, I was lucky enough to join one of Magnus's regular beginners' malt-tasting sessions at Gleneagles. The first malt he brought out was a Rosebank, a traditional lowland whisky, matured in a bourbon cask. Fellow taster Fiona Wilson and I 'nosed' it first, by gently swirling it round in the special, slightly bulbous glasses, and sniffing. The senses are immediately filled with the delicate, pungent aroma of fine malt. With the addition of distilled water (some connoisseurs will only use the actual water used by the distillery that produces the whisky), measuring about half the amount of whisky, you swirl and sniff again. This time there is a subtle change. It becomes smoother.

Our second whisky is a Speyside whisky, the Mortlach, which comes from a sherry cask. Again we swirl, sniff and taste, and our senses are delighted by a wonderful mix of caramel, chocolate and smoke. With the addition of water, the whisky tastes more strongly of smoke and oak.

The third and final whisky in our tasting session is Caol Ila, a malt produced from a bourbon cask, and which comes from the Isle of Islay. Islay malts have a very distinctive flavour, which you will either love or hate. Due to the high humidity and sea air they have a peaty, antiseptic aroma and tend to be something of an acquired taste. The ageing process with these whiskies is slower because of the high humidity levels.

A little while later, we have a last taste of the golden nectar and then depart for bed. The tasting ceremony has left us mellow and content. It is rather like a Japanese tea ceremony – the combination of ritual and instruction leaves you feeling you have taken one step closer to becoming a connoisseur of life. Malt whisky tasting is a civilised and infinitely warming activity, which gives a glow to any evening and leads to lively discussion about the tastes and smells of the golden liquid that swirls like a ballerina in your hand.

Two days later, having decided that we preferred the Rosebank and Mortlach to the Islay malt, we are ready for the intermediate tasting session. Magnus arrives with three more tempting bottles. As he says, 'The beginners tasting was to establish what you like. You need to know what you like so you can appreciate the better quality of the intermediate range malts.'

We have progressed from the standard bottle to a limited malt, which means that the whisky is made from specially selected casks and has lain in the cask for at least 17 years. (The standard malt has been in the cask for at least 12 years.)

First up is a 17-year-old Rosebank, which we can compare to the Rosebank tasted at the beginners' session. Once again, we swirl the malt round the glass and 'nose' it. It is quite a sweet, very smooth malt from a bourbon cask. Coming straight from the cask it is 63.9 per cent strength. This is really far too strong for enjoyable drinking, so the real art comes in adding exactly the right amount of distilled water to please the individual drinker.

The water, which is dribbled in and swirled around the glass, not only dilutes the malt, but brings out its full flavour. By the time we have added about double the water to the amount of whisky, the full flavour has been released and we have a

LAGAVULIN

perfect, light, slightly sweet honey malt that connoisseurs consider to be the leading lowland malt.

Our second bottle is an 18-year-old Mortlach. This comes from a sherry cask and has a cask strength of 63.1 per cent. This Mortlach has less of a chocolate and toffee flavour, and more of a woody taste. It is very smooth and full bodied.

Our final choice is the Royal Lochnagar – a very special malt whisky. The present Royal Lochnagar distillery was built by John Begg in 1845, on the Balmoral Estate, leased from Gordon of Abergeldy. Queen Victoria moved into Balmoral Castle in 1848. A few days later she visited the distillery at the invitation of the owner, accompanied by Prince Albert and a group of princes and princesses, all of whom tasted the whisky. Three days after this a royal warrant was granted on account of the excellence of the whisky.

The Royal Lochnagar is not cask strength (it is bottled after 12 years), but it is matured in a very superior oloroso sherry cask, which is hard to find. Elegant, smooth and very full bodied, the Royal Lochnagar is an ideal substitute for the after-dinner fine cognac. It is very smooth on the palate, and epitomises a great Highland malt whisky.

Nearly three days pass before we can find time to sit down to enjoy the advanced tasting. Here we have the jewels in the Highland crown, the single cask malts which are bottled from just one cask. Generally, one cask will supply about 200 bottles.

Our first whisky is a 22-year-old Benrinnes. This is a Speyside malt with a cask strength of 53.6 per cent. It is matured in a bourbon cask. Undiluted, the malt has a hint of wood and vanilla. Diluted the taste becomes very interesting indeed. There is still the hint of vanilla, but also another subtle aroma, which is difficult to define. It adds depth and mystique to a great whisky. As Magnus explains, 'It could be a new stave of wood in the cask that was used to replace a broken piece. This is the kind of unexpected thing that can create a truly great whisky, and that is the excitement of tasting new malts. Sometimes, you get the unexpected. You can't analyse exactly what it is – you just know it adds an extra dimension to a whisky which is already great.' The Benrinnes is very smooth, and has great depth of style.

Our second whisky is a lowland whisky which comes from the Bladnoch distillery. The cask strength is 57.9 per cent. It is 17 years old, but matures more quickly than other malts of the same age. It comes from a bourbon cask, but has a deeper colour than usual, which could indicate a first filling. When neat it has a vanilla nose, which changes to a traditional lowland nose when diluted with water. It has crisp, citrus, floral notes and is deliciously smooth.

Finally, we're on to a 21-year-old Caol Ila. This Caol Ila has a cask strength of 59.9 per cent and, again, it is matured in a bourbon cask. It is an Isle of Islay malt, but the antiseptic bite of the first Caol Ila we sampled is no longer dominant and the taste is much rounder and smoother. Because of the humidity, the malt matures slowly – it takes 28 years to become as mature as most other malts do in 21 years. On the 'nose' it smells better undiluted than diluted. Diluted, the Caol Ila becomes sharper in tone and more peaty. It is, however, eminently drinkable and a very good after-dinner malt.

TALISKER

101

OBAN

Fillet of Beef

STUFFED WITH SMOKED OYSTER ON FRIED CHANTERELLE MUSHROOMS WITH SAUCE FOYOT

4 x 170 g/6 oz beef fillet steaks

4 smoked oysters

4 large basil leaves

a little vegetable oil

30 g/1½ oz shallots, diced

50 ml/1¾ fl oz red wine

100 ml/3¾ fl oz beef stock

400 g/14 oz dry potato purée

nutmeg

a little flour

50 g/2 oz butter

200 g/7 oz chanterelle mushrooms

400 g/14 oz baby asparagus

salt and pepper

Sauce foyot

50 ml/1¾ fl oz reduced beef stock

200 ml/6¾ fl oz thick Béarnaise sauce

This is a variation on a traditional recipe called a Carpet Bagger.

❖

INSERT A SMALL KNIFE into the side of each steak and move from side to side to make a small pocket. Wrap each oyster in a basil leaf and push into the pocket. Heat a little vegetable oil in a heavy-based frying pan and seal the steaks on all sides, then cook to the desired degree. Remove the steaks and keep them warm.

Deglaze the pan by sweating the shallots for 2 minutes then adding the red wine. Cook for 1 minute then add the beef stock, bring to the boil and strain.

To make the potato purée, boil the potatoes until cooked, drain until completely dry, then add a little salt and pepper. Season the potato purée with the nutmeg and roll out to about 12 x 0.5 cm/5 x ¼ inch thick – you may need a little flour to firm the mixture up. Using a 12 cm/5 inch cutter, stamp out 4 circles and fry in 25 g/1 oz of the

butter until golden brown. Place one circle on each plate, browned side up.

Clean the chanterelles and then sauté them in the remaining butter in a heavy pan, over a high heat until just wilted. Cook the baby asparagus briefly in a little boiling, salted water. Drain well and add a little butter. Arrange the chanterelles and asparagus neatly on each potato circle, place a fillet steak on top and pour over the reduced wine and stock mixture.

For the sauce foyot, add the reduced beef stock to the Béarnaise and serve separately in a sauce boat.

Serves 4

Good accompaniment:
Cragganmore malt whisky, 12 years old

THE MALTS

The lowland malts make the best pre-dinner drinks, while the Isle of Islay malts are a superb after-dinner tipple.

104

MATURED IN SUPERIOR CASKS

Generally, one cask will supply about 200 bottles of fine malt whisky.

In general, the lowland malts make good pre-dinner drinks and the Islays are better after-dinner tipples.

Whisky connoisseur and leading world expert Charles MacLean, who wrote the definitive book on malt called, simply, *Malt Whisky*, is greatly encouraged by the move to produce malt and food as combined entities rather than as separate items.

'Malt whisky is a surprisingly good accompaniment to a broad range of foods and can make a happy contribution to the preparation of many dishes. There are no rules about which malt to drink with which dish. Experimentation is the order of the day! Malt whisky is a natural companion to smoked fish and meat, haggis (Talisker is my preferred choice with haggis), fruit cake and mince pies,' he says.

Once confined to the upper classes, who would have a 'nip' after dinner or as a prelude to hunting and shooting, malt whisky is now a popular drink with the discerning, younger generation. They are looking for the rare and unusual, and to satisfy that demand, Gleneagles holds malt whisky auctions, which have become very popular. A 1910 Rosebank will go for between £500 and £800, and a 1922 White Horse for between £400 and £600.

As Charles MacLean says, 'About five or six years ago, Christies began to hold auctions dedicated to whisky. Previously, the whisky auctions were just lumped in with wine auctions.'

Sothebys also take over the hotel for a week and people come from all over the world to buy the unusual malts offered up for auction. It is an occasion of real theatre – a man walks out with an apron on, holding a silver tray on which the bottle of malt proudly sits.

'People often ask me what to do when buying at an auction,' says Charles. 'My advice would be that if you come across a malt you like, particularly if it is a limited edition, buy three bottles; one to drink, one to keep, and one to auction. After a few years the last will have paid for the first two.'

THE STILL ROOM

*I*F THE MENFOLK are exhausted by the taxing business of purchasing gifts for their loved ones, they can drift into their own paradise. The Still Room is the malt lover's Garden of Eden.

John Miller runs the shop and loves his job. The Americans are his best clients. They purchase bottles of malt such as the Royal Lochnagar selected reserve, as special gifts for loved ones, or to enjoy themselves when they return home and are pining for the sweet tastes and images of Gleneagles. Recapturing the warmth of that Gleneagles welcome can be as simple as opening a bottle of malt whisky. Just shut your eyes and let the liquid gently soothe your tired soul, as you relive the happy memories.

The Classic Six malts are the most popular and well known (below):

Gordon Bell of United Distillers and Vintners (UDV) spends his working life as an ambassador for malt, travelling the world and promoting malt whisky – surely a job millions would envy. 'It's more of an educational job than a sales job,' he says, 'as we are informing people on the subtle differences between the malts. I must admit I love my job – nothing can beat settling down with a book and a glass of malt at the end of the day. As it is very much linked with Scotland, I think that malt whisky spreads a generic message about our beautiful country as well as about the product itself.'

Gordon has noticed the consumer is becoming more discerning. 'I spend three months of the year in the US, as well as extended periods in other parts of the world, and have noticed that people have become much more inquisitive about malt.

'Consumers are beginning to understand that malt whisky is as diverse a drink as wine. There is a far greater awareness of cask strengths and single cask malts, and people are increasingly able to recognise the difference between a sherry cask and a bourbon cask.

'I think the Classic Malts series helped create general interest and an

awareness of regional differences in malts. People now realise it is all right to add water to a standard malt. Of course, with the cask strength malts, the water brings out the full flavour. People learn how much water will give the taste they prefer.'

Gordon sees a bright future for malts. 'Consumers are experimenting more and malt whisky will go from strength to strength as a result. Bars now realise that if they have a good selection of malts, and a knowledgeable barman, they will improve their image. There is huge worldwide interest in Scotland, and malt is part of this. The film 'Braveheart' actually did wonders for Scotland's popularity. The misty, romantic image of the glens is very much in tune with the warming, magical feeling one gets from malt.'

PRODUCT	AGE	STRENGTH	AROMA/TASTE
Glenkinchie	10 years old	43% vol	Clean aroma
Lowland			Smooth taste, hint of dryness
Cragganmore	12 years old	40% vol	Firm body, dry aroma
Highland – Speyside			Malty, smoky finish
Dalwhinnie	15 years old	43% vol	Heathery finish
Highland – Northern			Light taste with a fruity, sweet aroma
Oban	14 years old	43% vol	Delicate hint of peat
Highland – Western			Long smooth finish
Talisker	10 years old	45.8% vol	Well balanced with a slightly sweet aroma
Island – Isle of Skye			Full flavour explodes on palate
Lagavulin	16 years old	43% vol	Heavy, powerful aroma
Island – Isle of Islay			Smoky peaty taste

BURNS' NIGHT

RABBIE BURNS

106

Rabbie Burns is Scotland's most famous writer and poet. In spite of his tragically short life (he was born on the 25th of January 1759 at Alloway, in Ayrshire, and died on the 21st of July 1796 at Dumfries, aged just 37), his poems, songs and writings have lived on and become a treasured part of Scottish culture.

Martin Treacher is a Glaswegian of many musical talents and is the person in charge of masterminding the celebrations for Burns' Night at Gleneagles. In Martin's eyes, Rabbie Burns has done more than anyone else in the history of Scotland to preserve Scottish songs.

'He often wrote poems with music in mind, and he rescued songs written by others, such as 'Coming thro' the Rye', and dressed them up,' says Martin. 'The entertainment we organise for groups is very popular, and an excellent way for people to participate and enjoy an evening dedicated to the extraordinary talent of Rabbie Burns.'

To start the meal, one of the guests usually recites the famous Selkirk Grace:

Some hae meat and canna eat,
And some wad eat that want it;
But we hae meat and we can eat,
And sae the Lord be thankit.

Then comes the Burns traditional Scottish supper – a four or five course meal. The menu below comes from Charles MacLean.

Menu

COCK-A-LEEKIE SOUP
(chicken broth with leeks)
HAGGIS WI' BASHED NEEPS AND CHAMPIT TATTIES
(haggis, mashed swedes, creamed potato)
Whisky: **LAGAVULIN**

ROAST RIB OF ABERDEEN ANGUS BEEF
(with Yorkshire pudding, roast potatoes, vegetables and thick gravy)
Whisky: **DALWHINNIE** *or* **GLENKINCHIE**

SCOTCH TRIFLE
(a rich sponge, custard and cream layered pudding)
Whisky: **TALISKER**

During the meal there is also much traditional reading and singing. When the haggis arrives the lights are dimmed, and it is carried ceremoniously in to the sounds of pipes, accompanied by the chef. Someone will be brandishing two bottles of whisky, which represent the antennae of an animal.

It is a great piece of theatre and very much enjoyed by all the guests. A special poem by Rabbie Burns is read:

ADDRESS TO A HAGGIS

Fair fa' your honest, sonsie face,
Great chieftain o' the puddin-race!
Aboon them a' ye tak your place,
 Painch, tripe, or thairm:
Weel are ye wordy of a grace,
 As lang's my arm.

The groaning trencher there ye fill,
Your hurdies like a distant hill,
Your pin wad help to mend a mill
 In time o' need,
While thro' your pores the dews distil
 Like amber bead.

His knife see rustic Labour dight,
An' cut ye up wi' ready slight,
Trenching your gushing entrails bright,
 Like onie ditch;
And then, O what a glorious sight,
 Warm-reekin, rich!

Then, horn for horn, they stretch an'
 strive:
Deil tak the hindmost, on they drive,
Till a' their weel-swall'd kytes belyve
 Are bent like drums;
Then auld Guidman, maist like to rive,
 'Bethankit!' hums.

Is ther that owre his French ragout,
Or olio that wad staw a sow,
Or Fricassee wad mak her spew
 Wi' perfect sconner,
Looks down wi' sneering, scornfu' view
 On sic a dinner?

Poor devil! see him owre his trash,
As feckless as a wither'd rash,
His spindle shank a guid whip-lash,
 His nieve a nit;
Thro' bluidy flood or field to dash,
 O how unfit!

But mark the Rustic haggis-fed,
The trembling earth resounds his tread,
Clap in his walie nieve a blade,
 He'll make it whissle;
An' legs, an' arms, an' heads will sned
 Like taps o' thrissle.

Ye Pow'rs, wha mak mankind your care,
And dish them out their bill o' fare,
Auld Scotland wants nae skinking ware,
 That jaups in luggies;
But, if ye wish her gratfu' prayer,
 Gie her a Haggis!

For the rest of the meal, the celebrations are accompanied by piano playing, the tunes of a wandering minstrel, or other background music. Between courses various entertainers perform songs by Rabbie Burns.

Rabbie Burns was a great whisky lover and there is plenty of whisky tasting included in a Burns' evening. Traditionally Burns' nights were male-dominated affairs, with all the men drinking and standing to recite poems and speeches. At Gleneagles the focus tends to be more on the music, and the 'Address to a Haggis' is usually recited by an attractive female singer.

The Haggis

WITH MARBLED CLAPSHOTT AND VEGETABLE CRISPS

2 sheets spring roll pastry
or filo pastry

1 small egg, beaten

1 tsp snipped chives

2 sprigs fresh thyme

25 g/1 oz melted butter

150 ml/¼ pint beef stock

1 shot whisky

2 tbsp double cream

salt and pepper to taste

220 g/8 oz haggis in skin

100 g/4 oz swede purée, made with
a little butter and milk

100 g/4 oz potato purée, made
with a little butter and milk

Vegetable crisps

1 carrot

1 beetroot

½ turnip

vegetable oil, for deep-frying

Haggis is the most traditional of all Scottish dishes. Here we have taken the haggis as our base and added some texture and colour to the dish. We will serve it as a starter with the traditional clapshott, a mixture of swede and potato.

PREHEAT the oven to 180°C/350°F/gas mark 4. Place one layer of the spring roll or filo pastry onto a board and brush with the beaten egg. Sprinkle on a few snipped chives and thyme and cover with the second sheet of pastry. Using a round cutter, cut out four 6 cm/2½ inch rounds. Cut down one side of each round to make a straight edge. Brush the rounds with melted butter and bake in the oven until crisp and golden brown – about 4 minutes.

Place the beef stock in a pan with the whisky, bring to the boil and reduce by two-thirds. Add the cream and correct the seasoning. Keep the sauce warm.

To make the vegetable crisps, slice the vegetables very thinly – if you have a mandolin this produces the best result. Heat the vegetable oil and deep-fry the carrot, beetroot and turnip separately for 2–3 minutes until lightly coloured and crispy, then leave to drain on kitchen paper. This can be done in advance and the crisps stored in a airtight container.

To assemble the dish, heat the haggis and spoon a little onto each plate. Lightly mix together the swede and potato purées to form a marbling effect and spoon this mixture onto the plates. Place some of the vegetable crisps and a pastry round onto each plate with the flat side of the pastry round in the haggis. Drizzle with some of the sauce and serve.

Serves 4

Good accompaniment:
Your favourite whisky

When Martin Treacher is not in Scotland, he is often involved in promotional tours, where he represents Gleneagles to top musical establishments in the USA and other countries. 'These events are like being welcomed into your own house party,' he says. 'Rabbie Burns' music goes straight to the heart, and there is a very warm and homely atmosphere. People can enjoy the taste of malt whiskies from the Classic Malt collection, and these are always very popular. We invite guests to sing solos – always a good way of getting people involved and breaking the ice at the party!'

Rabbie Burns spent the last few years of his life as an exciseman, trying to stop illegal whisky-making and smuggling. This brought about a certain conflict in him, which he expressed in a famous song, 'The Deil's Awa' Wi' the Exciseman', which is also usually included in a Gleneagles Burns' Night:

COMING THRO' THE RYE
Tune: Miller's Wedding

Chorus
O Jenny's a' weet, poor body,
Jenny's seldom dry:
She draigl't a' her petticoatie,
Comin thro' the rye!

Comin thro' the rye, poor body,
Comin thro' the rye,
She draigl't a' her petticoatie,
Comin thro' the rye!

Gin a body meet a body
Comin thro' the rye,
Gin a body kiss a body,
Need a body cry?

Gin a body meet a body
Comin thro' the glen,
Gin a body kiss a body,
Need the warld ken?

Gin a body meet a body
Comin thro' the grain;
Gin a body kiss a body,
The thing's a body's ain.

The Deil cam fiddlin through the town,
And he danc'd awa' wi' th' Exciseman,
And ilka wife cries:– 'Auld Mahoun,
I wish you luck o' the prize, man!

We'll mak our maut, and we'll brew our drink,
We'll laugh, sing, and rejoice, man,
And monie braw thanks to the meikle black Deil,
That danc'd awa' wi' th' Exciseman.

There's threesome reels, there's foursome reels,
There's hornpipes and strathspeys, man.
But the ae best dance ere cam to the land
Was the Deil's Awa' wi' th' Exciseman.

PIPING IN THE HAGGIS

CHRISTMAS AND HOGMANAY

Gleneagles has always known how to celebrate in style. Combine this know-how with the magic of Christmas – frosty, starry nights; feasts fit for a king; log fires, dancing, carol singing and a whole host of other activities – and you have a recipe for fantastic festive entertainment. And all in the luxury of one of the finest hotels in the world. Gleneagles is a magical place at this time of year. Snow is often falling, and makes for a stunning and beautiful landscape.

Christmas is a special time for children and teenagers and at Gleneagles they will be royally entertained. As well as staging traditional events, such as the arrival of Father Christmas, the hotel always chooses a special theme for its younger guests. In 1998 it was the circus, and the children received a 'fantasy world' pass, allowing them entry into the Gleneagles Fantasy World. The children also participated in a pageant organised by the staff and presented it, to the great appreciation of their parents, on Boxing Day afternoon.

Once the celebrations for Christmas itself are over, guests have a few days' rest before preparing for Hogmanay. Hogmanay has become established as one of the classic events in the Gleneagles calendar and a time when the legendary Scottish hospitality really comes into its own. Hogmanay at Gleneagles is much like a country-house party for honoured and cared for guests. From the moment they are welcomed by the Gleneagles piper, the guests are charmed by the infectious high spirits of The Highlands, revelling in an atmosphere that draws them back year after year. The millennium end-of-year celebrations promise to be extra special (see Chapter 8).

Hogmanay is also a great occasion for making new friends. The range of activities on offer at the hotel tends to bring people together, as guests receive instruction in shooting, riding, wine tasting, malt whisky tasting, Scottish dancing or gambling at the Casino School, while the kids have fun in the kitchens or participate in special themed events.

The Scottish appetite for the good life is seductive and is at its most irresistible during the festive season. And with the enigmatic scenery of the Highlands as a backdrop, guests soon begin to relax and let the warmth of Christmas and Hogmanay fill their hearts, minds and spirits.

111

A TRADITIONAL CHRISTMAS
What better setting than The Gleneagles Hotel to enjoy a traditonal family Christmas?

THE WEDDING

O N THE 25TH OF JULY 1992 Lt Colonel Ron Smith's daughter, Catriona, got married at Dunblane Cathedral. The reception was held at The Gleneagles Hotel, and it was an occasion that the Smith family will never forget.

'It was the first time I had really experienced being a guest at Gleneagles. On that day I didn't think of the staff as hotel colleagues, I thought of them simply as my friends – friends who were trying to make my daughter's day the best ever. The staff treat everyone in that way, but it was really brought home to me how much they care for guests and friends alike.'

Catriona is a principle soprano with the Stuttgart Opera and her Irish husband, Paul McCann, is a tenor. As the couple are based in Germany, all the arrangements for their wedding service and reception had to be made long distance.

The wedding was a very typical Scottish wedding, which had been lovingly arranged by her parents. After the service, which was conducted by

Colin MacKintosh, Catriona and Paul were chauffeur-driven to the Gleneagles Hotel in a Jaguar.

'I had arranged for the car to drive Catriona to the front gate and then for a horse and carriage to take her and Paul to the front door,' remembers Colonel Smith. 'But what I didn't know was that Peter Lederer would be positioned at the front door with Neil the piper, waiting to greet the bride and groom. Quite a few guests were also there to see her arrive. It was raining and cold, but the hotel guests always love a wedding, as does everyone, and we managed to turn a blind eye to the weather. I think an occasion such as this lifts the spirits, and having my daughter's wedding at Gleneagles was very special.'

As Catriona and Paul are both singers, there was not surprisingly a strong musical theme to the wedding. In fact, their friends doubled up as the

choir for the service in Dunblane Cathedral.

'All the wedding supplies were provided locally,' explains the Colonel. 'We had a local florist, as well as the hotel florist, and the printing of the wedding service and menu was carried out by a local printer. Ian Ironside baked the cake, which was magnificent, and we had a ceilidh band that I had seen playing in the hotel.

'After the traditional welcome at the ballroom entrance, we were seated for the meal and listened to the speeches.'

The bride and groom cut the cake with Colonel Smith's sword, which was a 1914 vintage Royal Artillery sword which he bought for £5 in 1956. Today such a sword would set you back about £700. Colonel Smith had the sword restored in the 1970s and now proudly brings it out for weddings and other joyous occasions.

Wedding Menu

Ogen melon with summer berries

Supreme of chicken with toasted oatmeal and whisky sauce

Market vegetables and potatoes

Bitter chocolate mousse with compote of cherries

Coffee and petits fours

'The children at the wedding were all spirited away and entertained for several hours by some very kind and competent ladies,' says Colonel Smithl. 'This meant that the adults had the freedom of the room, which made things a bit easier for serving food and getting down to enjoying ourselves.'

Catriona has her own special memories of her wedding day. 'Having a father who worked at the best hotel in Scotland was definitely a bonus when it came to wedding plans. The effortless organisation by the various members of The Gleneagles Hotel team made it all run very smoothly.

'The day before the wedding, I was treated to a facial and manicure at the Spa. That was certainly very relaxing and

calming and I felt I was ready for the big occasion.

'The service was lovely and, being passionate about music ourselves, we chose the music for our wedding very carefully. It was a damp and chilly day, but the greeting we received at Gleneagles from Peter Lederer and Neil the piper made us forget the weather. We felt very special.

'After the photographs had been taken and we had welcomed all the guests we were finally permitted our first glass of champagne, which was much needed by that time. We glided down the stairs and into the ballroom to great applause.

'After that, everything seemed to rush by. The waiters did a fantastic job

keeping the wine flowing and making sure everyone was happy, and we danced the evening away with Scottish and Irish reels and jigs. We finally finished partying around midnight, after a hectic few hours' dancing. It was a day I'll never forget.

'When the reception was over we didn't have too far to go. We just jumped into the hotel Range Rover and drove round to the back entrance. We walked through the kitchens and up to our suite, room 215, which is a well-known honeymoon suite.

'The suite was fantastic, although unfortunately some of our friends had got in there first. So I only hope Housekeeping weren't too overworked the following day!'

THE CHILDREN ARE OUR FUTURE

'Here's to the child and all he has to teach us.'

ANCIENT PROVERB

As we reach the end of the century, our hopes and dreams are focused on what the new millennium might bring. The guests who visited the hotel in the 1920s are now in their eighties and nineties. Many of them have brought their children and grandchildren to visit the 'Highland Palace in the Glen'. Now the future belongs to today's children, who will bring their partners and families to the hotel during the next century.

In the 1920s children were most definitely to be seen and not heard. Things have changed, and now the small people are welcomed and treated as valued

JUNIOR GOLF
It's never too early to start and with a few lessons from the club professional, any one of these young children could develop into a new golf star.

Gleneagles guests. Diana Scott has been employed by the hotel to develop the family side of the marketing brief, and this means entertainment. If the children are kept busy then mum and dad can relax and enjoy themselves. Gleneagles knows that many of their guests are families who come year after year, and that children will develop friendships one year that they will want to rekindle the next. In 1997 there were 1,000 more nights of children's occupancy than in 1996, and this trend is continuing.

Diana gathers information on school term times from all over the UK. Term times differ between England and Scotland, and in Northern Ireland they are different again. Diana distributes this information to the different hotel teams, from the kitchens to housekeeping, and the respective teams prepare a list of activities for children to do during the holidays. A highly successful activities week took place during the summer of 1998 with hockey, football and rugby proving the most popular pastimes.

But the fun really starts at Reception, where the kids receive their welcome packs. A disposable camera and a photo album for the over fives, and a story book, colouring book, crayons and a soft ball for the under fives. A newsletter is produced for the 'Young Eagles' (as the young Gleneagles regulars are called), and if any child has a birthday which falls during their stay, then they are sure to receive a card.

As Diana says, 'We always try to think in advance and provide as many activities as possible. We can supply pushchairs, nappies, sterilising equipment, and special foods. We want to make life as easy as possible for the parents, so they can truly enjoy their holiday.'

For Christmas and Hogmanay 1997 the conference rooms were converted into a circus. The children were given circus passes for three days, which allowed entry into the Big Top to learn tricks, watch tightrope walking and juggling, and see puppet shows. At the end of the three days the children put on a show for their parents and grandparents.

The Easter Sunday Easter egg hunt is legendary. The fun starts with the hunt in the morning, carries on through the day, ending with the party in the evening.

There are plenty of activities to enjoy outside the festive season too. A particularly successful initiative is the 'own a pony' day, where children look after one of The Equestrian Centre ponies for a day, as if it were their own. They collect the pony from the field, groom it, have a lesson, then remove the tackle and feed it. After they have fed the pony, and had some lunch themselves, the children spend the afternoon listening to a talk on stable management and taking part in a pony quiz, to see what they have learnt. The whole experience is rounded off with a prize-giving ceremony of rosettes and certificates.

A similar activity is available at The Golf Academy, where the children enjoy a junior golf lesson. On arrival, they are taken to study the 'Young Gun fitting gauge', a simple chart which tells you at a glance the right size club for a particular child. The smallest club is around 2 feet long. Children's clubs are relatively inexpensive, with prices starting at around £14 for an iron and £10 for a putter. The Academy's youngest ever golfer was 18 months old.

The children then have a swing session, which is recorded on video. In an attempt to encourage youngsters to try the game, the Gleneagles top-rated team of teaching professionals have produced a very special educational pack – for £20 the children receive a souvenir photo and a 30-minute lesson. For £30 they get the same, but also a new club, to encourage them to keep playing the game when they have left Gleneagles.

The British School of Falconry allows children of four years and above to handle the birds and become familiar with them. The Off Road Driving School is also a great favourite. Obviously, children are not permitted to drive the vehicles themselves, but they love watching their parents getting stuck in the mud and doing battle with the water and steep slopes.

If the little ones are still full of energy after all this, they can be shipped off to the Shooting School to participate in archery, air rifle shooting or clay pigeon shooting, depending on their age and ability. And if that doesn't wear them out, then there's mountain biking, pitch and putt, a children's round on the Wee Course, tennis, croquet, football, basketball, rollerblading and, of course, The Club, which not only has a lap pool for the more serious swimmers, but also an outdoor hot pool, a volcano pool, and a Jacuzzi.

For the more cerebral youngster, the playroom is being revamped to offer a range of computing facilities. Children will be able to experiment with e-mail, computer games and Sony Playstation.

GOLF SCHOOL
Some of the hotel's younger guests take a turn at mastering the art of falconry.

115

Children's Recipes

Children and cooking are always a recipe for fun, as long as it's under the watchful eye of one of our trained chefs. Here are some dishes prepared in our popular Kiddies' Kitchen sessions.

Florentine Biscuits

For the sweet paste

375 g/13 oz butter

100 g/4 oz caster sugar

3 egg whites

500 g/1 lb 2 oz plain flour

1 small egg

For the florentine mixture

220 g/8 oz butter

450 g/1 lb caster sugar

100 ml/3¾ fl oz honey

90 g/3½ oz chopped glacé cherries

90 g/3½ oz chopped angelica

200 g/7 oz sultanas

140 g/5 oz currants

350 g/12 oz flaked almonds

100 ml/3¾ fl oz double cream

100 g/4 oz dark chocolate, melted

FOR THE SWEET PASTE, cream together the butter and sugar until light and fluffy, then gradually add the egg white. Fold in the flour. Place in the fridge to become firm, then roll out to approximately 5 mm x 30 x 20 cm/¼ in thick x 8 x 6 in. Cook on 180°C/350°F/gas mark 4 for approximately 10 minutes without colouring.

Place the butter and sugar in a pan and cook until almost toffee like. Add the honey and blend in. Add the cherries, angelica, sultanas, currants and flaked almonds and mix thoroughly, then stir in the cream.

Pour the Florentine mixture on to the cooked sweet paste and spread evenly. Place back in the oven and cook for 15 minutes at 180°C/350°F/gas mark 4.

When the Florentine biscuits are cool cut into the desired shape. Brush the base of the biscuit with the melted dark chocolate. Allow to cool and serve.

Makes 16 good-sized biscuits

Flapjacks

250 g/9 oz butter

250 g/9 oz soft brown sugar

150 ml/¼ pint golden syrup

500 g/1 lb 2 oz rolled oats

PREHEAT THE OVEN to 180°C/350°F/gas mark 4. Melt the butter and add the soft brown sugar and golden syrup. Keep on a low heat until the sugar dissolves – do not boil. Remove from the heat and add the oats. Place on a baking tray 30 x 20 cm/12 x 8 in and roll the mixture to 2.5 cm/1 inch thick. Bake for approximately 15-20 minutes. Allow to cool and then cut into squares.

OPPOSITE: *Mince pies, florentines, fairy cakes and flapjacks never fail to please the younger generation.*

THE GROUNDS AND THE TERRACES

Lawrence Gorlas is the man who runs the Gleneagles gardens and estates. He has worked at the hotel for 22 years and has not only developed and maintained the stunning gardens, but also set up an independent business that operates under the control of Gleneagles. In 1994, Lawrence looked at the possibility of becoming self-sufficient and making the gardening side of Gleneagles into a consultancy, which would offer expert advice to companies and individuals who might be designing a garden, or simply seeking advice. Lawrence's business is enjoying considerable success.

But back to the beginning. The gardens were first designed in the 1920s by G S Carter, a company of landscape gardeners from Glasgow who charged 1,500 guineas to design the gardens – a huge amount at the time. With harsh winters and windswept summers, the estate was a demanding one to plan. At Gleneagles, the wind comes from the west and blows across the front of the hotel, so it was necessary to create a screen of trees in order to protect the buildings and the borders of shrubs and seasonal flowers.

The gardens display a subtle difference in style according to location – more formal close to the hotel and less so by the Dormy Clubhouse and golf courses. Linking the two areas are the famous 'Golden Path Steps'.

All the beds are seasonal. Bedding plants such as geraniums, begonias, fuchsias, lobelia and cineraria brighten the pathways and provide a warm welcome for the guests in the summer. Then in winter pansies and polyanthus take over, while bulbs such as daffodils and tulips are planted to provide colour in the spring. The gardens contain some very old trees and plants, such as the 75-year-old Virginia Creeper, and many interesting trees such as the *Liriodendron*, or tulip tree, which is a newer addition in The Club.

For Lawrence, gardening is a passion as well as a job. He is justifiably proud of his team, who work all year round to provide guests with a stunning carpet of visual splendour on which to feast their eyes as they arrive at the gates of the Scottish estate. The bedding plants are changed from year to year to ensure that regular guests always have variety.

For the Gorlas family, Gleneagles is in the blood. Lawrence's father worked as a chef at the hotel, his mother as a cleaner and his sister in housekeeping. He met his wife Lorraine at Gleneagles too. She used to serve champagne in the Braids

GROUND WORK
Lawrence Gorlas, Head Gardener, looks on as two of his team tend plants in one of the estate's large greenhouses.

Champagne Bar and went on to become head of one of the bars. Lawrence began his own Gleneagles career as an apprentice chef, largely to please his dad, but found he was not cut out for the chef's life and, after three years in the Black Watch, he rejoined Gleneagles as an apprentice gardener. 'Gleneagles is my life,' he says. 'The place gets to you. You fall in love with it and become totally immersed. If a guest makes a complaint you always want to put it right. It's really important to us that guests have good things to say about the different aspects of the hotel.'

Lawrence and his groundspeople have been a key success factor in many Gleneagles events – the first Bell's Scottish Open Championship in 1987 was a particular triumph. Two hundred and twenty flowers were spread throughout the tented village, and flower beds were planted especially for the occasion. Everyone admired the beautiful grounds and there were drinks all round to celebrate.

IN THE COMPANY OF FRIENDS

One of the features of The Gleneagles Hotel that is continually commented on by guests is the extraordinary family atmosphere and the close and warm relationships between staff. When hotel favourite Billy Lynch suffered a particularly traumatic time a few years ago, the hotel offered him support and protection. 'During a personal crisis, I was ready to give up my job and uproot,' explains Billy. 'Peter Lederer called me up to his office for a chat. He said, "Billy, I might be the Managing Director of Gleneagles Hotel, but you're Mr Gleneagles. I'm not going to lose you. If you feel a bit down, come up and have a cup of coffee. My door is always open." Mr Lederer is a marvellous man. He and George Graham gave me tremendous support when I needed help to get my life back on track.

'I can see myself here until I retire. I've already received a watch for 35 years' service and if I stay until I'm 65 that will make 47 years' service – I can't see anyone beating that.

There's only one thing I object to here, and that's the casual dress. I like to see men properly dressed with a tie on in the evening. It's all very well going into a pub wearing a jumper or open shirt, but not a 5-star hotel.'

One occasion when the guests would really get dressed up was the annual dinner for the gathering of the 51st Highland Division. The men would eat in the dining room, and the women in the lounge. There were some great characters, who would gather from all over the UK, and beyond. The person in charge was Major Campbell. Every night Billy would have to fix Major Campbell's bow tie, to make sure he was properly dressed. The major would say, 'Billy, would you like a wee snifter?' and Billy would join him for a glass of whisky in the sitting room.

Many years ago, when the Duke of Argyll was going through a very messy divorce, the major was most put out, as he felt the Duke was letting down the Campbell name. Billy takes up the story, 'He said to me, "What do you make of the Duke getting divorced and disgracing the name of Campbell?" He wouldn't stop talking about it – he was obsessed with the shame the divorce brought upon his name. Suddenly, there was a knock on the door, and in walked the Duke of Argyll. "Campbell, is everything ready for tonight?" asked the Duke. "Oh yes, your Grace," the Major replied, "Billy is just making sure my bow tie is tied correctly." "Right Campbell, I'll see you later," said the Duke and went out the door. As soon as he was out of sight, the major was off again, "Billy, what do you make of him disgracing the clan?"'

Billy's career at Gleneagles would probably make him the perfect diplomat, should he ever wish to leave his beloved hotel. He is constantly called upon to sort out some of the more delicate problems that arise, sometimes with the four-legged variety of friend. 'When I was a pageboy,' Billy recalls, 'the Head Porter said to me one day, "Right Lynch, go up to room 110 and take the labrador for a walk." Off I went. The dog made straight for the lamppost on the left-hand side of the hotel entrance, lifted its leg and ... well, there must have been a wire loose or something, because it sparked. It took me about four hours to find that dog!'

THE COLONEL ARRIVES

In 1984, Peter Lederer decided a rather special person was needed to act as the main point of contact with the guests. The guests wanted 90 per cent of Peter's time, and he wanted to give it, but other matters needed attention. He decided to appoint a dedicated person who would be able to give the guests all the attention they needed. This is how Lt Colonel Ron Smith arrived on the Gleneagles scene.

The Colonel was a breath of fresh air. A professional soldier, who had served queen and country for over 30 years in the army, Colonel Smith had reached 50 and was looking for a new challenge. One day, an advertisement in *The Scotsman* caught his eye. It read: 'Peter Lederer, General Manager of Gleneagles Hotel, requires a Guest Services Manager. The function of this post is to represent him personally to the guests. It is unlikely that a candidate of under 45 years would have the right experience for this post. It might suit a service officer.'

The Colonel was intrigued. He applied for the job and attended an interview. This was followed by a further interview, with the then Managing Director of Gleneagles Hotels plc, Peter Tyrie. The Colonel was offered the job in the autumn of 1984 and took up his post on the 12th of February 1985. 'When I asked Peter Lederer what I would do, he replied, "That's up to you. It's you who will be representing me. You have to make up the job. It doesn't exist yet."

'As I began to get used to representing the management to the guests,' the Colonel continues, 'I found I was actually doing something else, which was representing the guests to the management. I could see Peter Lederer's logic. I wasn't a hotelier, I was independent, and that's what the hotel needed – someone who wouldn't always tow the party line, but would see things from the guests' point of view as well. In computing terms, I was the interface between the guests and the management, meeting, greeting and keeping my eyes and ears open, so that if something required attention I could pick up the phone and act on it.'

For Colonel Smith it wasn't a pain-free adjustment. Rather than bark out orders military style, he had to get used to relying on diplomacy to persuade people to take on his ideas. His vast international experience in the development of new weapons systems for the army was important, as it had given him vital

THE ROYAL FAMILY AT GLENEAGLES

*T*HE WINDSORS have come in for much criticism over recent years, from press and public alike, but at Gleneagles the British Royal Family is always regarded as part of the hotel's extended family, particularly Princess Anne, the Princess Royal, who is about as down-to-earth and relaxed as it is possible for a Royal to be.

Princess Anne has become quite a regular at Gleneagles. One year she was at the hotel when it was her daughter Zara's birthday.

As the occasion coincided with an evening function, Zara asked Chris de Burgh to sing his famous song, 'Lady in Red' for her, and he was more than happy to oblige.

The following day Helen Stewart, Jackie Stewart's wife, was taking Zara back to school, and as she was about to leave, the Princess Royal appeared on the stairs with a large box which read 'Fragile. Zara Phillips' Birthday Cake'.

As Billy Lynch says, 'It's nice to see that Princess Anne can enjoy being an ordinary mum here without anyone bothering her.'

Billy also has special memories of when Princess Alexandra visited the hotel with the Lord Lieutenant of Perth, following a public engagement. The princess did not return to the

Princess Anne with Peter Lederer

hotel for another six years, but always remembered Billy. Her husband, The Honourable Angus Ogilvy, used to say to him, 'She sends her regards, Billy.'

The human touch means a lot to the staff who look after the Royals and other VIPs who visit Gleneagles.

experience in industry, government procedures and sales and marketing, all of which he could now bring to his new career. He knew he had made an impression when he remarked to a guest, 'I am not a professional hotelier,' and the guest replied, 'No, but you are a professional gentleman.'

The Colonel arrived around the time of the takeover of Gleneagles by Arthur Bell & Sons plc in 1984, and things were still a little unsettled. Some staff had left and Peter Lederer was building up a strong management team which included Sheila Perera, the Executive Housekeeper, and George Graham, now the General Manager, who are still there today. The Colonel's first impression of the hotel was that it was 'grand and somewhat unwelcoming,' sentiments echoed by his wife. Now he considers it a happy home, where standards are always high.

It was the Colonel's job to set up the guest history on the new computer system. This database detailed all the likes and dislikes of the guests. For someone with a military background, this was easy to organise as it was in essence an intelligence-gathering exercise. 'A hotel isn't so different to the army,' explains the

OFFICIAL
GREETING
Lt Colonel Ron Smith
greets Michael Parkinson.

Colonel. 'It feeds people, provides accommodation, transport, leisure facilities and finds solutions to problems.'

The international experience he gained during his army career also helped Colonel Smith create a bond with guests from more far-flung corners. Having lived in America, he could say to guests, 'Oh, you're from St. Louis. Have you been up the Arch?' and talk meaningfully to them about their homeland.

The army training also came in useful one January in the early 1990s, when everyone was snowed in. The Colonel arrived for work at 8.00 am on Monday and left at 6.00 pm on the Wednesday! The A9 was blocked with 600 vehicles from Braco to Auchterarder. You could get to Auchterarder but no further. 'We had an American Express event in house,' remembers the Colonel, 'and the guests were trapped. The entertainment that night was a mini-Highland games, so we had all these muscular guys in kilts wandering around – it was very odd! We were also taking in guests who were trapped in their cars and sending out our four-wheel vehicles to rescue the unfortunate. I had brought a pair of wellies, a sweater and a pair of old army trousers. Sheila Perera supplied underwear from Auchterarder, and we had plenty of white shirts in the laundry room.

'It felt like we were back in the days of wartime rationing, with the dining room forced to limit the portions of food it could give out, as the staff were unsure how long the situation would last. It could have gone on for four or five days. We also reduced the room rates, as we didn't think it was fair to take advantage of people stuck in the snow.'

Ron Smith was born in Dunblane and married his wife Isobel in Dunblane Cathedral. When he came to Gleneagles he came home. 'The guests are very special people,' he says, 'which is why they are called guests, not clients, customers or punters. They are guests in our home. Gleneagles is our home. It may be our working home but it is still our home, and we welcome guests into our home.'

THE GLENEAGLES DIPLOMACY

Regular guest Clare Smith (no relation) has become a VIP in her own right at Gleneagles. She first fell in love with the hotel in 1984, when she decided to celebrate her retirement from teaching there. 'It was planned as a one-off stay,' says Clare, 'but was the start of an enduring love affair. As the car that had picked me up from the airport went through the gates and started up the drive, my heart began to beat very fast. I was excited, but scared, and wondered what I had let myself in for. Gleneagles was used to welcoming royalty, millionaires and celebrities. Surely the staff would look down upon an elderly, homely, far from rich ex-teacher. I was wrong. Immediately I felt the warmth of a true welcome, a feeling difficult to describe yet utterly real. I felt completely at home. My stay was blissful.

'As I sat in the front hall filling in the hotel questionnaire on the last morning of my stay, a young man came along and we began to chat. In the course of our conversation I discovered he was the General Manager. I ticked "excellent" on almost every section of the questionnaire, but couldn't resist writing a comment in the space provided. I wrote, "But you don't know how to cook kippers." I like my kippers poached and the ones I had for breakfast had been grilled. When I returned home and told my husband what I had written he was appalled. "Seventy chefs and you have the nerve to tell them they can't cook kippers!" I had a nice letter from Peter Lederer. He explained that I cook kippers the English way and they cook them the traditional Scottish way. A perfect, diplomatic reply.'

Another Gleneagles regular, Mrs Andreis, is a great fan of Colonel Smith. From the time she first stayed at the hotel in 1991, she was aware of the Colonel's special gift for making everyone feel at home. 'My son liked the Gleneagles tie, but it was sold out in the shop. Colonel Smith got to hear of this, and the next evening there was a Gleneagles tie lying on the bed. He wouldn't accept any payment; it was given with the compliments of Gleneagles. He was always willing, helpful and smiling. All the staff are so friendly. I'd call it a home from home, but that would be to underestimate its luxury. I couldn't bear ever having to give up Gleneagles,' says Mrs Andreis.

The Gleneagles diplomacy and discretion certain impressed Sir Neil and Lady MacFarlane when they booked into the hotel for a quiet weekend in 1985.

Arthur Bell and Sons plc had just been acquired by Guinness plc and the then Chairman was Sir Norman MacFarlane. Sir Neil and Lady MacFarlane were astounded when they arrived and were shown into the most magnificent suite in the hotel, with a stunning view over the glorious Glendevon. As they were unpacking, the housekeeper arrived to enquire if everything was to their liking. 'We were very surprised, having booked an ordinary room, to be shown into this palace of a suite,' says Lady MacFarlane. 'After a while, we realised that they thought my husband was in fact Sir Norman. To the hotel's eternal credit, they kept us in the suite and didn't change a thing. I call that service with style. We have stayed at Gleneagles regularly ever since and, as our wedding anniversary is in January, we often spend the New Year there. It is quiet, but always nice and cosy. We always try and make at least two or three trips to Gleneagles a year.'

It is clear that the appointment of Lt Colonel Ron Smith as a member of staff dedicated solely to attending to the needs of the guests was an excellent move for Gleneagles. The Colonel retired in February 1997, but is still a familiar figure at the hotel. He retains a highly positive view of life. 'I have had four lives,' he says, 'Childhood and School. The Army. The Gleneagles Hotel and now Retirement.' The Colonel is not short of things to keep him busy during his retirement. He is the honorary treasurer of the Oz 99 Tour, which is the summer 1999 tour to Australia of the Queen Victoria School in Dunblane, and has a number of other projects up his sleeve. 'I set out a plan when I retired and I haven't even touched some of the things yet,' he confesses.

CHAPTER SIX

Golf at Gleneagles

'If heaven is as good as this,
I sure hope they have some
tee times left.'

LEE TREVINO ON HIS FIRST ENCOUNTER
WITH THE GLENEAGLES GOLF COURSES

L EE TREVINO, the great American golfer, left no-one in any doubt as to what he thought of Gleneagles, and almost every amateur and professional to have played on the courses have echoed his sentiments.

Three internationally renowned golf courses – The King's, The Queen's and The Monarch's – cover a considerable area of the hotel grounds. The courses stand on a natural moorland plateau of some 700 acres. Majestic pines frame the fairways and give perspective to the stunning views enjoyed by the golfers. The Ochil Hills to the east and the south are split by the dramatic Glendevon Valley, and to the north and west lie the Grampians and the Trossachs. Banks of yellow gorse and, in late summer, heather clothe the hills in glorious purple. Wildlife abounds to distract the golfers from their game, as their world of pars, birdies and bogeys is invaded by grouse, hawks, buzzards, wild geese, pheasants, partridges, deer and hares. It has been known for the odd Harris' Hawk to get confused and mistake the golf club for its lure!

James Braid, the greatest golf course architect of his day, was commissioned to build The King's and Queen's Courses just before the First World War and Gleneagles proved to be the place his genius blossomed. There can be few stretches of land better suited to the construction of golf courses, but it took a shrewd eye and even more imagination to prise out such remarkable layouts from the land in the days when the spade, shovel, and horse and cart were the only equipment available.

The Gleneagles courses, although not by the sea, resemble the older links courses in Scotland in that they are built on sand and gravel, which were deposited when the last ice sheet finally melted

OPPOSITE:
THE PERFECT
SETTING
The gently rolling
Ochil Hills surrounding
The King's Course provide
a stunning backdrop to a
round of golf.

124

some 15,000 years ago and left long ridges, flat-topped mounds and enclosed hollows. Braid turned this dramatic landscape into The King's and Queen's Courses. The result is an idyllic golfing landscape where many of the fairways and greens, particularly on The King's, are isolated from neighbouring holes by the gravel ridges, so giving golfers the luxury of feeling they are playing on their own private course. The turf on these older courses is firm and springy and therefore never tiring to play on.

By the 1950s, The King's, The Queen's and the Wee Course had been constructed. In 1974 the Wee Course was renamed The Prince's and doubled its size from 9 to 18 holes. In 1980 a new 18-hole golf course was built and christened The Glendevon.

When Jack Nicklaus built The Monarch's and it was decided to scrap The Prince's and The Glendevon. The Prince's reverted to being the nine-hole Wee Course. Gleneagles therefore now boasts four magnificent courses, making it a truly unique place to play golf.

James Braid was not only the greatest golf architect of his day, as creator of the magnificent King's and Queen's Courses, but also the greatest player of his generation, winning the Open Championship five times. It was totally appropriate, then, that a new course at Gleneagles should be designed by the golfer who succeeded Braid as the greatest of his particular generation – Jack Nicklaus.

MONARCH'S

Jack Nicklaus tees off at the star-studded opening of The Monarch's Course.

126

A NEW ARRIVAL

When The Monarch's Course was unveiled in May 1993, the unanimous opinion was that Jack Nicklaus had matched the achievements of Braid. The King's and The Queen's had a bright, new, precocious younger brother. Yet the opening of The Monarch's Course was nearly called off due to snow – unusual in May, even by the standards of The Highlands. Linkman Billy Lynch remembers the Duke of York arriving for the opening. 'The weather was awful. The Duke of York came up the driveway in his Jaguar, with his detective in the passenger seat. He came round the roundabout the wrong way, stopped right in front of the steps, got out and went straight into the hotel. Then he burst out laughing and said, "Do you think I'm daft. If I'd driven round the right way, I'd have had to walk all the way round the car and would be soaking by now. I took the short cut!"'

Fortunately, the opening did go ahead as planned, although the round was shortened. Jackie Stewart was playing with The Duke of York, Jack Nicklaus and Sean Connery, and much to his regret, he lost a pound on a bet! 'We had a pound on which pair would win,' remembers Jackie. 'Unfortunately for Sean and me, The Duke of York and Jack Nicklaus won on the 18th hole with a long putt sunk by the Prince. And that was bye-bye to my pound!'

Singer Chris de Burgh has a special memory of the opening of The Monarch's Course. 'I was in the last four ball to tee off, and surrounded by what felt like hundreds of spectators, television cameras and press photographers. I was the last to go in a party that included Kenny Dalglish and Princess Anne's husband, Commander Tim Laurence. To say that my legs felt like jelly is an understatement. I'm quite happy to sing in front of 100,000 people but playing golf in front of 100 is a horrifying experience.

'Fortunately, I hit my drive straight down the fairway, slightly to the left. My caddy, a dour Scotsman, handed me a five-iron and gestured towards the elevated tee. "Give it a whack," he said, so I gave it a whack and the ball disappeared out of sight. There was a rather feeble cheer from the onlookers around the flag, which I could not even see. When I got to the green, I could see three balls on the green, two near the fringe and one about eight inches from the pin. Naturally, I assumed that my ball was on the fringe, but I was astounded to be told it was the one nearest the pin. I tapped it in for a birdie.

'Outside I remained perfectly calm, as if this sort of thing happened every day, but inside I was jumping up and down like an excited child! That was a great memory of Gleneagles.'

Regular guest Clare Smith also has fond memories of the day The Monarch's Course was opened. 'In 1993, I was a guest at the opening of The Monarch's Course,' she recalls. 'My husband had just died and it was a wonderful event that gave me a boost during a difficult time. I was thrilled at the prospect of seeing Jack Nicklaus, whom I have admired for many years. I was over the moon when I was introduced to the great man and had my photograph taken with him. I spoke to Prince Andrew, Mary Parkinson, Eamonn Holmes, Gene Hackman and Sean Connery. It was a great day and in the evening £250,000 was raised for charity.'

**PRACTICE
MAKES PERFECT**
*Golfers of whatever level
of ability can put the
finishing gloss on their
tee shots and putts in the
Academy.*

A PRIVILEGED CLUB

Membership gives you access to five different golfing clubs at Gleneagles. The Dun Whinny, named after the first tee on The King's Course, was formed in 1936 and is the most traditional and conservative of the clubs. Then there's the Dun Ochil and the Dun Bracken. This latter is the ladies' club, the members of which are charmingly referred to as the 'wicked witches of the west' by the male club members. The men claim they know when the ladies are out by the broomsticks lined up outside the Dormy Clubhouse! The other two clubs are the Glenearn and the Gleneagles Golf Club. The Gleneagles Golf Club alone has 140 members.

In the old days, golfing refreshments at the Dormy Clubhouse would consist of morning coffee and biscuits, a three-course meal around lunch time and 'high tea' – typically ham and eggs or fish and chips – in the afternoon. Now the menu caters for more eclectic tastes and in summer the restaurant is open from 9.00 am to whenever the last guest wishes to leave.

THE KING'S COURSE

James Braid's brief for building The King's Course was simple. He was told: 'Make it spectacular, make it look difficult, but make it easy to get round.' Braid's new course was a triumph, though from the back championship tees only the most skilful players would regard it as easy. The King's Course is generally considered the leading course at Gleneagles, largely because it hosts the McDonalds' Women's PGA Championship of Europe and for eight years hosted the Bells' Scottish Open. Braid designed The Queen's Course at the same time as The King's, but the former originally had only nine holes. Shortly after the hotel opened, it was decided to extend The Queen's Course to eighteen holes.

Braid's clever use of the ridges at Gleneagles has produced a classic golf course. The typical hole on The King's Course invites the golfer to hit a drive from an elevated tee into a valley with a few strategically placed bunkers, before facing a tough shot to a plateau green which falls away in all directions into deep bunkers or thick rough. Selecting the right club for each approach shot is probably the secret of playing The King's Course successfully.

The King's has only one hole that could be described as flat (the 10th), so there is a premium on being able to manufacture shots that find a way of negotiating the natural obstacles. With the golf course standing at 600 feet above sea level, there is always likely to be a breeze, generally from the west, to confuse calculations. And there's not much let up once you reach the greens either – the slopes are easy to see but difficult to master. A slight miscalculation of line or pace and a putt can end up 10 feet from the hole. In the summer the greens play lightning fast.

Braid sometimes used the ridges to produce blind shots, and these are a feature of golf at Gleneagles, more common on The King's than on The Queen's. Blind shots are unfashionable now, but they were the norm in the early 20th century, when The King's Course was built, and they certainly add an unusual quality to the play. With King's, familiarity with the course is the key to playing a competent round. Nearly everybody underestimates the distances required to hit the raised greens when they are playing at Gleneagles for the first time. The optical illusion caused by the immense expanse of land and sky, and the clear light, makes the fairways seem shorter than they are and tends to result in the ball being played short. A good caddy can help to remedy this.

A ROUND ON THE KING'S COURSE

All the holes on the Gleneagles courses have been christened with evocative and colourful Scottish names.

1st – Dun Whinny, 362 yds, par 4

They say an opening hole should always whet the golfer's appetite for the test ahead, and not be too demanding. The wide fairway here will encourage even the inexperienced golfer. Dun Whinny is the name of the gorse-covered slopes at the right of the plateau green. The green slopes steeply from back to front.

2nd – East Neuk, 436 yds, par 4

Neuk is the Scottish word for corner and this hole reaches the most easterly point of The King's Course. The hole bends round to the left, with the green positioned 60 ft lower than the tee. The green on East Neuk usually plays extremely fast and slopes from right to left. To get your shot as close to the pin as possible you need to aim for the right side of the green. Unfortunately this is where a cavernous bunker awaits the slightly mishit shot.

3rd – Silver Tassie, 374 yds, par 4

The name refers to the cup-shaped hollow beside the silver birches that grace this green. The tee shot is uphill into a valley full of heaving mounds and hollows. The second shot is totally blind, over a huge hill protected by the Dougal Cratur bunker. The green is so big that placement of the pin can make a difference of between two or three clubs.

4th – Broomy Law, 466 yds, par 4

One of the toughest holes on the course, usually played into the wind, and named after the broom bushes covering the 'law' or hill to the right-hand side of the hole. A sloping fairway tends to throw everything into the rough on the left. The green is 40 ft higher than the tee.

5th – Het Girdle, 178 yds, par 3

The green is long and narrow and sits high on a raised plateau, although it is actually only 5 ft higher than the elevated tee. The name means 'Hot Griddle' and refers to the fact that poorly hit golf balls will slip off the green just as oil slides off a hot plate.

6th – Blink Bonnie, 480 yds, par 5

This means 'beautiful view', so called because of the shining waters of Carsebreck Loch and the peak of Ben Lomond that can be viewed in the distance. Blink Bonnie is a fairly straightforward long hole, the main problem being to select a tee shot which is able to clear the saddle of ground and bunkers situated about 270 yds from the tee.

7th – Kittle Kink, 444 yds, par 4

This means 'Tricky Bend' – an appropriate name for this sharp dogleg left. The tee shot has to clear a downward slope in the ground called 'The Little Rig'. Getting to the green is only half the problem; the large green is half an acre in size and has a pronounced serpentine-shaped ridge running through it to test even the most skilful shot maker.

8th – Whaup's Nest, 178 yds, par 3

OPPOSITE:
**THE 17TH,
WARSLIN' LEA**

The tee stands high above a lochan known as 'The Black Water'. The tee shot is hit to an inviting green in the shape of a curlew's (or whaup's) nest, situated 20 ft below, over a heather-covered gully.

TOM WATSON – STARTER ON THE KING'S COURSE

TOM WATSON is the popular starter on The King's Course. The players see him as a friend, as well as a member of the Gleneagles staff. Guests or club members who come to play on The King's Course are often beset with last-minute nerves at the thought of making total idiots of themselves on the famous course. Tom, with his gentle sense of humour and calm demeanour, helps them settle.

'The players come from all over the world and they arrive here with great expectations. I'm lucky as I'm on the first tee, where everyone's still in a good mood. Meeting some of them when they come off the 18th tee is quite a different matter!

'As soon as I spot the players walking towards me, I can tell that they are excited about playing on one of the world's most beautiful courses. I always try to make sure they get a good start.'

Tom knows that The King's is the number one choice for a lot of people and it is his job to ensure that everyone who wants a game is able to get on the course. 'I pull out all the stops to get everyone in. I don't like to think that people come here and fail to realise their dream.'

Tom is up at 5.30 am, starts work at 7.00 am, and finishes around 4.00 pm, when most people have teed off. His 'home' is a beautiful white hut with a Rolex clock on the top, and from there he watches the golfers tee-off every ten minutes. He has a screen with all the players' names on it for that day, and a card with the relevant information about each golfer, those new to The King's as well as those more familiar with the course.

Tom is a great golf lover who has played the game all his life. 'The King's Course is the primary attraction. It is beautifully designed by James Braid, who worked with the natural contours of ground to create it,' he says.

Tom has met many celebrities in his time. 'Prince Andrew is a keen golfer, and a very nice gentleman, and Commander Tim Laurence is also a keen and improving golf enthusiast.

But my one outstanding memory in the six years that I've been doing this is of Bob Hope and his wife, Dolores. I met them in June 1994, when Bob Hope was 91. He said to me, "Tom, are you up here everyday?" I said, "Yes sir, five days a week." "What a wonderful place to work," he enthused, to which I replied, "Well, the weather's not always so wonderful!" Then he said, "I have played on all the finest courses in all the finest golf resorts, and you work at the number one spot in the world." That really made me feel good about my job. He is a very special man.

'I remember when Neil Armstrong came to play. It took him so long to get organised on the first tee that his three friends said, "If you'd taken that long in 1969, you'd never have got to the moon."'

Tom loves his job and the benefits it has brought him: 'It has enabled me to play at the world's finest golf clubs, thanks to invitations from people who have played here at The King's,' he says.

'I've played three rounds at Pinehurst Number 2, the venue for the 1999 US Open. It's a very difficult course, but I had an excellent caddy. Working at Gleneagles has opened doors for me. I hope to realise my dream of playing around the world – I particularly yearn to play at Pine Valley and Augusta. I consider myself very fortunate to be in this position. If I wasn't here then I would not have been able to revel in my "retirement" and enjoy such an interesting life. And I hope to play on for many years yet.'

9th – Heich 'o Fash, 409 yds, par 4

A classic King's Course hole, where the first shot needs to be hit from a high tee down into a valley, then up on to a raised green. The name means 'Height of Trouble', probably a reference to the two yawning bunkers that protect the two-tier green and which are extremely difficult to get out of successfully.

10th – Canty Lye, 499 yds, par 5

The name means 'Pleasant Meadow', which accurately describes a relatively flat, straightforward hole. It is in distinct contrast to the nine holes that have preceded it. The only real danger on the hole is if the ball is pulled too far left, where the ground slopes away steeply.

11th – Deil's Creel, 230 yds, par 3

Despite its name, which means 'Devil's Fishing Basket', the dangers here are not related to water, but to an arrangement of six tricky bunkers around the green. This green slopes from back to front and is very fast at the front.

12th – Tappit Hen, 442 yds, par 4

Another hole with a magnificent view of the Ochil Hills and Craig Rossie. A large ridge called 'The Muckle Rig' that has three bunkers in the face crosses the fairway at 200 yds to intimidate the golfer on the tee. The hole is named after a clump of trees behind the green which resemble a crested hen.

133

13th – Braid's Brawest, 464 yds, par 4

James Braid always signed his name to the hole he considered his best. The tee shot here has to be to the right or centre of the fairway to avoid 'Auld Nick's' bunker. The second shot is to a plateau green above the level of the player. The fairway narrows as it approaches a smallish green.

14th – Denty Den, 309 yds, par 4

'Dainty Dell' is one of the prettiest holes, with a small green protected by six bunkers and overlooked by an elegant spinney of Scots pines. The accuracy required to reach the green from the tee is so great that few take the risk.

15th – Howe o' Hope, 459 yds, par 4

At this stage of the round, a downhill hole that drops 60 ft from tee to green is much enjoyed by golfers, hence the name, 'Valley of Hope'. The main danger *en route* to the green is posed by the 'Hell's Holes' bunkers located in the middle of the fairway, around 120 yds from the pin.

16th – Wee Bogle, 158 yds, par 3

The 'Little Goblin' is the shortest hole on The King's Course, but it is by no means the easiest. There are a total of nine bunkers to catch the wayward shot – to the left, to the right and in front of the green. The green slopes from back to front and from left to right.

17th – Warslin' Lea, 377 yds, par 4

Warslin' means 'troublesome' and, although not a long hole, the 17th is a dogleg with the narrowest fairway on the course – many golfers take an iron to ensure they stay in play. The green is protected by bunkers and a steep slope at the front, so the second shot needs to be long.

18th – King's Hame, 525 yds, par 5

The home hole is a wonderfully welcoming one to finish with. The fairway drops 60 ft from tee to green, and big hitters who can clear 'Cairn Rig' from the tee will find their ball rolls down into two-shot range. The 18th green is the largest on the course. The front half is fast with severe borrows and the back half is flatter with more subtle slopes.

THE QUEEN'S COURSE

In today's game the top professional players, with their much-improved modern equipment, are able to hit the ball very long distances, with the result that The King's Course, being 825 yards longer from the championship tees than The Queen's, and 506 yards longer from the medal tees, has come to be regarded as Gleneagles' top course. But it is not everyone's favourite.

The Queen's Course is a friendlier and more picturesque course that has many fans. Trees attractively frame and define each green, and there are fewer blind spots. Arranged among high ridges, The Queen's delights the spectator with lovely woodland settings, small lochs and ditches.

The course's difficulties are similar to those facing the golfer on The King's – undulations, rough and natural bunkers – yet The Queen's has a feeling of more space, as the ups and downs of the terrain are not so severe. Three par 3s on the back nine plus par 4s of 252 yards and 318 yards make it quite a short return journey from the halfway house.

A ROUND ON THE QUEEN'S COURSE

1st – Trystin' Tree, 409 yds, par 4

A tricky start. The hole falls away from the tee then bends sharply left and uphill to a flat green. There are no bunkers close to the green – Trystin' Tree is one of only two greens on the course to be left unprotected. James Braid regarded this as the pick of the nine holes he designed. The name means 'Lovers Tree', but it is not entirely clear which is the tree in question.

2nd – Needle E'e, 146 yds, par 3

As the name implies, the tee shot needs to be threaded skilfully through the trees. The main challenge, however, is to successfully clear three massive bunkers located in the face of the raised green, and avoid falling away into the large hollow to the right of the green.

OPPOSITE:
**THE 13/14TH,
LOCH-AN-EERIE**

134

3rd – Gushet Rig, 421 yds, par 4

The name means 'Gushing Water in a Ploughman's Furrow', the furrow being the ditch to the right-hand side of the hole. A ditch and a large bunker eat into the left of the fairway at 230 yds, making it a very tight drive. The green is protected by 6 bunkers and several large clumps of gorse and pine.

4th – Warlock Knowe, 355 yds, par 4

This large, undulating green in a setting of broom and heather seems especially inviting once you have reached the fairway but, as with most of the greens at Gleneagles, it is on a raised plateau that will throw anything other than a perfectly hit shot into trouble. The name means 'Warlock Hill'.

5th – Glower O'er 'em, 177 yds, par 3

Braid's original 9-hole course turned back to the hotel after the 4th, so the current 5th is the first of the additional 9 that were built later on. The green is larger than it looks, but the high-lipped bunkers give the impression of a very small target.

6th – Drum Sichty, 437 yds, par 4

The views from this hole are particularly fine – the name means 'Sight of the Hills'. Out of bounds and bunkers down the right-hand side of the fairway make it essential to stay left. Another elevated green in the shadow of pine trees.

7th – Westlin' Wyne, 491 yds, par 5

The name means 'Winding Hole at the Most Western End of the Course'. It bends rather than doglegs. Westlin' Wyne is a fairly straightforward hole where it is better to stay to the right to get the best view of the green, which has a ridge running down the centre.

8th – Auld Fauld, 337 yds, par 4

The 'Sheep Pen'. A downhill, blind tee shot must avoid the massive bunker that protects the approach to the green, which nestles in a hollow. More wonderful views from here across to the neighbouring hills.

9th – Stey Brae, 419 yds, par 4

This means 'Steep Hill', and the name couldn't be more apt. A swinging dogleg right which requires the golfer to hit a long tee shot in order to see the green for the second shot. First-time golfers on The Queen's Course will inevitably leave their approaches short, sometimes by as much as two clubs.

10th – Pint Stoup, 421 yds, par 4

A fascinating hole where the green lies in a hollow behind two hillocks, with just a narrow entrance. The golfer must either fly the ball all the way to a fast green and hope it bites, or land it accurately in the gap from where it should run forward. The name means 'Pint Flagon'.

11th – Muir Tap, 318 yds, par 4

'Top of the Moor' is a relatively easy hole. There are five bunkers protecting the green for the second shot, but most players will be using a short iron.

12th – Tinkler's Gill, 433 yds, par 4

The drive must be placed as near as possible to the top of the slope, which is around 160 yds from the green, to have a chance of getting up in two. Bunkers and towering pines surround the green. The name means 'Tinker's Drink'.

13th – Water Kelpie, 140 yds, par 3

This means 'Water Sprite', and water is the dominant characteristic of this lovely hole alongside Loch-an-Eerie, at once picturesque and distracting. The loch eats into the right-hand side of the green and, inevitably, players tend to play into one of the two large bunkers short and left of the green in their determination to avoid a watery death.

14th – Witches' Bowster, 215 yds, par 3

The course now turns 90 degrees along the north side of the loch. This hole is named the 'Witches Pillow' after its two-tier raised green (there is a difference of five feet between the levels). With golfers needing a wood or a long iron, the water down the right-hand side is a threat, as are three large bunkers around the green.

15th – Leddy's Ain, 252 yds, par 4

The 'Lady's Own' is a hole which longer hitters will want to try to drive. If the two bunkers 175 yds off the tee can be avoided, then the shape of the green will

THE 18TH,
QUEEN'S HAME

tend to gather shots and leave a certain birdie, or perhaps even an eagle. However, trouble awaits any shot which leaks right, where the ground drops away into the Heuch o' Dule, a heather-covered valley running the entire length of the hole.

16th – Lovers' Gait, 378 yds, par 4

Before the course was built, this was reputed to be a favourite spot for courting couples, hence the name. A pleasant hole which drops 30 ft from tee to green, the natural hazards and springy turf have all the characteristics of a seaside course. The green can be the quickest on the course, but has deceiving borrows.

17th – Hinny Mune, 204 yds, par 3

A very tough par 3 to come to at this stage of the round. A long, thin green makes it a tiny target, and if you miss it you will end up either down a steep slope on the right, in trees on the left or in gorse beyond the green. No-one seems too sure if the name means 'Beautiful Moon' or 'Honeymoon'.

18th – Queen's Hame, 412 yds, par 4

The Queen's 18th tee offers a splendid panorama. The golfer looks out over a little bridge that crosses the small loch, Deuk Dubs, and on to the green and the distant hills. From the elevated back tees the drive needs to carry 180 yds to cross the water. This leaves a fairly safe shot to a large green.

THE MONARCH'S COURSE

The Monarch's has been hailed as a thoroughbred among golf courses. It is far enough from the championship tees to present a stiff challenge to the best players of the day, but has wider fairways and requires fewer blind shots, so is not too daunting for less experienced golfers. The difficulties Jack Nicklaus has created with this course are, for the most part, plain to see, and include four large American-style bunkers at strategic points. Overall, however, he has stuck to Scottish-style bunkers with big lips and a links feel.

The course is unusual in having five par 5s, five par 3s and eight par 4s. By building five tees at each hole, Nicklaus allows the golfer to pick the length of the course he or she wishes to play. This can vary from a massive 7,081 yards from the championship tees to a relaxed 5,065 yards from the red tees.

A ROUND ON THE MONARCH'S COURSE

1st – Bracken Brae, 426 yds, par 4

A pleasant opening hole, the green is narrow and angled across the line of the fairway, so forcing golfers going for the green to play across one of the massive American-style bunkers that protect the approach. The name means 'Fern Hill'.

2nd – Wester Greenwells, 516 yds, par 5

Named after a ruined croft on the hill to the right of the green. Few difficulties on

138

THE 9TH, CROOK O'MOSS

the fairway, but the fun begins when the green comes into view. Built on the edge of a lochan with five bunkers for extra protection, it forces anyone who wants to go for the green in two to hit not only long, but with extreme accuracy.

3rd – Schiehallion, 431 yds, par 4
Named after the famous 3,553 ft mountain to the northwest of the course, this is a dramatic dogleg right where the tee shot skirts water. The green, like most on The Monarch's, does not have the same ridges and undulations as the greens on The King's and Queen's Courses, but it does have subtle borrows which tends to make it difficult to read.

4th – Gowden Beastie, 239 yds, par 3
Named 'Golden Bear' after Jack Nicklaus (although many golfers will think the description could equally apply to the enormous bunker of golden sand on the left-hand side of the hole, which is comfortably bigger than the green). Unusually, the green has three tiers, rising from the front to the centre then falling away again at the rear.

5th – Crookit Cratur, 461 yds, par 4
One of the most difficult holes on The Monarch's. The brave will play left down the fairway, keeping out of the trees. This gives a straight shot to the green. If you go right with your drive, then your second shot must carry over the marsh, which protects the right-hand approach to the green. Only one bunker on this hole.

6th – Mickle Skelp, 194 yds, par 3

Called 'Small Hit', misleadingly so, since even from the medal tees the hole measures 168 yds. The tees are aligned to force the golfer to play over a large marsh. Anyone who attempts to play to the left in the hope of avoiding the marsh risks ending up in a deep bunker cut into the green.

7th – Larch Gait, 419 yds, par 4

The second shot here is one of the few blind shots on The Monarch's Course. The golfer must play over a ridge, which has 3 bunkers built into the face, to a large green without bunkers. Unlike the golf architects of 75 years ago, Nicklaus believes that if you are asking a golfer to play a blind shot it is unfair to confront him or her with hazards that cannot be seen. Named 'Larch Walk' after the splendid forest of larch to the left of the hole.

8th – Sidlin' Brows, 392 yds, par 4

This means 'Series of Undulations'. The main threat, however, comes not so much from the undulations as from a tricky narrowing of the fairway about 250 yds from the tee. The difficulties are made greater by a marsh to the right and a cluster of three bunkers to the left. Another split-level green.

9th – Crook o' Moss, 564 yds, par 5

The drive is over the water which gives the hole its name, but it is the approach to the green that can be terrifying if you are choosing a long shot. Depending on which route you choose, the approach can either be over the biggest bunker on the course, over a marsh or over a second expanse of water.

10th – Sleekit Howe, 208 yds, par 3

The name means 'Tricky Hollow'. The main threat is a large, deep bunker to the right of the green. The golfer gets a good view of all the problems from an elevated tee.

11th – Laich Burn, 350 yds, par 4

Named after the stream which for mere mortals dominates the second shot. Big hitters will probably take an iron from the tee to avoid their shots going right to the top of the hill, and trickling back down again into the burn. An undulating green, but one that should be quite easy to hit with a short iron.

12th – Carn Mairg, 503 yds, par 5

'Hill of Sorrow' features 13 bunkers, including another American-style monster on the direct route to the pin, to challenge anyone who is trying to get up in two.

13th – Wimplin' Wyne, 449 yds, par 4

'Meandering Turn' is a gentle dogleg. A cluster of 3 bunkers in the elbow needs to be avoided with the drive. Nicklaus' trick with this hole was to place the bunkers that protect the green 30 yds short, making judgement of distance difficult.

14th – Nebit Knowe, 196 yds, par 3

Named 'Pointed Hillock' after the large hill which overlooks the green to the left-hand side, Nebit Knowe is another hole where the green has been built across the line of the shot. This gives a very narrow target to aim at and very little space to stop the ball.

15th – Ochil Sicht, 463 yds, par 4

As the name 'Sight of the Ochils' suggests, this is an excellent place from which to view the magnificent Ochil Hills to the south. The golfer must play right off the tee to avoid a severe depression of rough, which runs for over 200 yds along the left-hand side of the hole. For those who play too safe, there is a large bunker awaiting at 240 yds.

16th – Lochan Loup, 543 yds, par 5

The fourth of the five par 5s on the course, 'Leap the Loch' is certainly the most picturesque and arguably the best. The small loch should stop all but the most powerful hitters from going for the green in two, and even those who do will still be left with a shot of around 150 yds over the water to hit the green in three. The name speaks for itself.

17th – Ca' Canny, 194 yds, par 3

The green on this hole is built in a hollow and from the back tee presents a small target, as a large bunker eats into the left-hand side of the green. There is a ridge running up the green which makes long putting difficult. At this late stage of the round, Ca' Canny is a tough par 3 to cope with, hence the name, which means 'Be Careful'.

18th – Dun Roamin', 533 yds, par 5

The last five holes on The Monarch's Course are not for the faint-hearted – a long, difficult stretch with two massive par 5s, two long par 3s and a dangerous par 4. The 18th is a sweeping dogleg right with yet another of the Nicklaus trademark greens, set at an angle to the fairway. A massive sand trap 80 yds from the green makes accuracy critical.

The Monarch's is a long course, certainly, but it has a great deal of charm and has won a host of admirers from those who have played on it.

As with The King's and Queen's, the unique feel, colours and views of the Gleneagles landscape make a round on the course one to savour. The Monarch's is already well on the way to becoming a highly established course and seems destined to achieve the same distinction as its two older neighbours.

Finally, we mustn't forget the Wee Course. This recalls the nine-hole course constructed in 1928 by the Gleneagles staff and head greenkeeper, George Alexander. The Wee Course is an excellent training ground on which to perfect the short game and practise skill and accuracy. It remains a strong favourite with guests and club members.

THE PROFESSIONALS

Gleneagles enjoys the reputation of being one of the world's great golf resorts. For eighty years, since just after the end of the First World War, and before the hotel was built, people have been playing golf at this magnificent place.

Given the high status of golf at Gleneagles, it's not surprising that there is keen competition to be the Resident Golf Professional. Ian Marchbank held this post for thirty years from 1962 to 1992, and during that time Gleneagles became a part of his life. 'The golf courses at Gleneagles have a magical feel to them. Everything has got to be perfect. When I played at Gleneagles it was always *my* golf course, and I felt proud to be a part of such a great name. Scotland is the home of golf and Gleneagles the Holy Grail,' he says.

Although Ian wasn't around when James Braid built The King's and Queen's Courses, he understands how incredible an achievement it was to design courses back then that are still regarded as championship standard today, when the game has moved on so much. In 1908 there weren't any bulldozers – Braid had to rely on men with picks, shovels, horses and carts. That is what has made the contours and feel of the courses so special.

Ian's father used to bring business associates to play at Gleneagles and at 14 Ian played his first round on The King's Course. In fact, golf had entered his soul a lot earlier – as a child, he would be given 2d by his mother to play 9 holes of golf on the municipal course, which was a stone's throw from their house. It was the start of a great love affair with the game, and the prelude to an incredible life spent meeting and playing with some of the greatest golf celebrities of the day, as well as some of the true characters of the game, most of whom were caddies. In the 1950s and 1960s, caddies were a breed apart and, in Ian's words, 'usually unemployed and unemployable'.

IAN MARCHBANK

143

GREG SCHOFIELD

144

Tam the Goose was one such character, so called because he wore a feather in his hat. Tam was an eccentric old caddy who, between 1952 and 1974, would lead golfers round the courses, making sure they all got the best out of their game. He lived in a residence for the homeless in Perth and would catch the bus or hitchhike to Gleneagles, arriving in an old raincoat and six sweaters. Or sometimes he would pitch a tent under a tree on what is now The Monarch's Course. Sadly, Tam the Goose met his maker when he suffocated after putting a charcoal brazier in the shed.

Ian also remembers another old caddy who, like Tam the Goose, was known for his eccentricity. Mahoney, or Dublin to his friends, was still caddying at 83. He would caddy for the same people each year, and once they'd finished their golf for the season he'd tell them he was retiring to London to be with his daughter. That way he'd get an extra tip. The following year Dublin would appear again and tell his customers he'd come back especially for them! As Ian says, 'People caught on, but no-one objected. It was seen as part of the game.'

Ian has played golf with a whole host of celebrities. 'Sean Connery came to play after filming 'Goldfinger'. He is a very nice man and now an excellent golfer. The 1960s and 1970s were very much the era of the celebrity golfer. Bing Crosby came up with his son Nathaniel. Once the press leaked news of the visit, a group of middle-aged ladies laid siege to Gleneagles, clutching autograph books and record albums. Bing spent half an hour with them before playing his round. And they were virtually all still there when he came off the course.'

Greg Schofield is the present Head Golf Professional at Gleneagles. Greg puts in a long day, from 7.00 am to 8.00 pm, but has a job that anyone with a passion for golf would envy.

The game of golf has been transformed over the past few decades. Golf in the 1990s has fewer characters, more facilities and demands a more technical approach. At Gleneagles the emphasis is on corporate days and group events, and the caddies are provided and managed by The Caddy Company (see page 149). There is a caddy passport training scheme, which one cannot imagine Tam the Goose or Dublin taking seriously.

Golf is now cited as an antidote to that great 1990s disease, stress. As Greg says, 'The pros tend to get on the courses when most of the members and guests have finished. If it's been a bad day or you've had a tough phone call, bashing a few balls on the range is a great way to relieve stress.'

Although 44 per cent of the golf played at Gleneagles is on The King's Course, Greg admits that for him The King's is his weakest course. His favourite is The Monarch's, followed by The Queen's.

Greg knows how special his job is. Apart from the fabulous facilities, he has come into contact with people he would never have met if it weren't for his work. 'Playing with Sean Connery was a special thrill. Not too many people can claim to have played golf with James Bond! Sean Connery is a good golfer and extremely fit. You can easily mistake him for a far younger man.'

One of Greg's few qualms is that royalty have an unfair advantage on the golf course. 'Prince Andrew is an excellent seven handicap player, but I think his two bodyguards are worth at least two shots a round. If he hits the ball off the tee and it goes wide off line into the rough, he has two extra people to find it. Everyone should have bodyguards on the golf course.'

THE TROPHY ROOM

Gleneagles has held many golf tournaments and the Trophy Room is certainly an impressive place. A large room located in the Dormy Clubhouse, it houses trophies from as far back as the 1921 pre-Ryder Cup Challenge.

Bell's Scottish Open
The Bell's Scottish Open was played between 1987 and 1994. It was one of the most successful competitions of the modern game and drew enormous crowds to Gleneagles. On the Dormy Clubhouse wall are the pictures of the famous winners. They are: 1987 Ian Woosnam; 1988 Barry Lane; 1989 Michael Allen; 1990 Ian Woosnam; 1991 Craig Parry; 1992 Peter O'Malley; 1993 Jesper Parnevik; 1994 Carl Mason.

The Silver Tassie
This is probably Gleneagles' most historic trophy. First played in 1925, The Silver Tassie was open to all golf club members with a handicap of four or less and includes a scratch and a handicap section. It is certainly the oldest trophy, but has not been played every year – it was suspended during the Second World War, and in the late 1980s had to be put on hold because the increasingly sophisticated amateur circuit meant that the top players had too much pressure on their time. Gleneagles is hoping that at some point the Silver Tassie can be reinstated.

THE SILVER TASSIE

The McDonalds' Women's PGA Championship of Europe
This is currently the most famous championship played at Gleneagles. It is one of the highlights of the European women's professional tour and is played over The King's Course in August. The splendid design on the trophy shows a pair of hands being lifted into the air, with the inscription, 'helping to lift children to a better future'.

The Platinum Trophy
This is one of the most unusual trophies, showing an eagle with a platinum golf ball in its claws. The tournament is an annual two-day championship run by Gleneagles for American Express platinum card holders.

The Monarch's Challenge Trophy
This was played just once, as part of a lavish ceremony to mark the opening of The Monarch's Course in May 1993. Kenny Dalglish's team won the trophy.

DEVELOPING THE GOLF TRADITION

With such fine courses and such a highly concentrated area of expertise to call on, it was only natural that Gleneagles would seek to sell its golfing services to the outside world.

Gleneagles Golf Developments (GGD) was created with this goal in mind. It is a wholly owned division of Gleneagles plc and, not surprisingly, Gleneagles is its primary client.

Managing Director Ian Ferrier travels the world as an official representative of Gleneagles, promoting golf and looking at new investment opportunities and ways of expanding the operation. Working with Gleneagles certainly opens doors, as the name is held in high regard in golf circles, and represents the ultimate in quality and style.

The company specialises in three areas – golf course design, golf management and golf marketing. It has projects in four continents, in locations as diverse as Bahrain, Katmandu, Delhi, Sicily, Sardinia, Rome, Tuscany, Majorca and Cape Town.

Jimmy Kidd is Director of Turf Grass Management at GGD and is an expert on grass and various other playing surfaces. At 22, Jimmy became the youngest ever Head Greenkeeper at Glasgow Golf Club, which is the world's fifth oldest golf club, and he has met some of the all-time greats of golf, including the man who built The Monarch's Course, Jack Nicklaus. 'I remember one year when the midges on the course were so bad that Jack was forced to take up smoking again to kill them off. He and his caddy, Dave McIntyre, had to smoke to avoid getting bitten,' recalls Jimmy.

Jimmy's son David is the Design Director and is currently designing the company's first US-based links golf course in Oregon. GGD manages the only grass course in Bahrain and has just opened one in Majorca.

Golf course owners are always keen to use the Gleneagles name and enjoy the enhanced status this brings, but GGD has strict criteria on who can qualify for this. Development Director David Dean is responsible for responding to such enquiries. His main objective is to protect the brand name and traditional image of golf, but in some areas concessions have been made.

One example is golf carts. Golf carts were always frowned upon in Scotland as being an American habit, but are now allowed on The Monarch's Course in recognition of the fact that some of the more elderly golfers have problems walking round all 18 holes. 'Making people feel comfortable is only logical,' explains Ian Ferrier. 'We are looking at providing valet parking so that golfers can at least start their game dry.'

Ian feels privileged to have met so many great golfing faces in the course of his work. 'Gene Hackman was great,' he says. 'Very intelligent, well read and gentle, not at all like his movie roles.'

A few years ago, Ian came close to realising a lifelong dream. 'It was at a time when I'd ruptured my Achilles' tendon and was forced to hop around the office. I came into my office one day and there was a fax from Jack Nicklaus on my desk. It read, "Would you like to join me for a game of golf? I'll be over in May." I

THE BUSINESS OF GOLF
Ian Ferrier and Jimmy Kidd discuss plans for a new international golf course.

worked out that I'd still be in plaster. I couldn't believe it. He was my childhood hero and I'd always dreamt of playing golf with him, and now I couldn't. My colleagues had to block their ears as I let out a stream of expletives! Everyone knew about my misfortune.

'One day I was in the middle of telling Jackie Stewart the sad tale when I heard a noise outside the office. I opened the door and there they all were falling about laughing. It had all been a joke. They'd sent me a false fax, and I'd been completely taken in.

'Some time later, I was cutting the grass at home when my son came out to tell me that Jack Nicklaus was on the phone. Naturally, I thought the pranksters were out again. I told him not to wind me up, but went through to pick up the phone to see who the joker was. It was Jack. He'd failed to make the cut at Muirfield and asked if I could play golf with him.

'The problem was that I was due to go on a family holiday the next day and family holidays are sacred. My wife would have murdered me if I'd delayed the holiday, so I had to turn the game with Jack down, much to my disappointment. I didn't break the news to my wife until we were well on the way to our holiday destination. "Are you insane?" she said. "You turned down Jack Nicklaus?" It seems it just wasn't meant to be.'

Jimmy Kidd has his own memories of well-known sportsmen. 'I was driving Mark Phillips around the grounds one day,' remembers Jimmy, 'and he kept hopping out and opening the gates. After about eleven gates, Peter Lederer, who was in the back, tapped me on the shoulder and said, "I think it's wrong to ask Princess Anne's husband to get out and open gates." After this, I opened the window and shouted, "Would you hurry up there, please." "There goes your knighthood," said Peter.'

THE MCDONALDS' WOMEN'S PGA CHAMPIONSHIP OF EUROPE

WOMEN'S GOLF has come a long way since the women's tour began in 1979 and top players like Laura Davies have made it an interesting and exciting game to watch. The inaugural year for the McDonalds' Women's PGA Championship of Europe was 1996. Television audiences for the tournament are growing – it can be seen on BBC Scotland or live on the cable TV channel, Eurosport. And if the cricket is rained off it gets national coverage in the UK. At least 40 to 50 journalists cover the event and over 50,000 spectators attend the 4 days – a number which is increasing annually. The tournament is based on the McDonalds' Open in the US, which has been running for 18 years and has raised over £29 million.

Catherine Panton Lewis is the tournament's Executive Director. It is a job which gives her great satisfaction, not only from an organisational point of view, but also because all the proceeds go to charity – the Ronald McDonald House Charities (Europe). The charity funds projects to build houses close to hospitals, so that parents can have a home from home when they are visiting their sick children. In the UK there are Ronald McDonald houses near Yorkhill Hospital in Glasgow, Alder Hey Hospital in Liverpool and Guy's Hospital in London. In total there are 197 Ronald

McDonald houses in 16 different countries across the world.

In the UK over £1 million has been raised in 3 years at the multi-sponsored event. The 200 or more guest sponsors, who are accommodated at the hotel for the duration of the championship, also have their own tournament, played over 3 days. On the first day they play with the amateurs on The Monarch's Course, and on the second and third days they play with the women professionals on The King's and Queen's Courses.

'A lot of people work together to make this event successful,' says Catherine. 'We have over one thousand volunteers and Ford supply us with courtesy cars. Without the help of sponsors we couldn't possibly raise the same sums. We sell anything we can to sponsors – space on the caddies' bibs, signs, space on the course. Even the 'quiet please' paddles are sponsored.

'In the 'volunteers' village' you can grab a hamburger, soft drink, coffee or a doughnut. We always give a party for the volunteers, who enjoy themselves in

their 'uniform' of T-shirts and caps. Volunteering is very popular with the ladies who participate in the event,' says Catherine.

There have been some lighter moments. 'We had two lady volunteers picking up litter on The Monarch's Course,' remembers Catherine. 'They commented on how clean it was, and were rather pleased with their undemanding workload – until we pointed out the tournament was on The King's Course!

'We had a bit of a stressful time in 1997 when British Airways were changing their computer system at Heathrow's Terminal 4. They managed to lose just about all the luggage and a few golfers turned up with no clubs. We eventually retrieved it all, even if some people did only receive their luggage the day before they were leaving.

'Another time we ran out of food on the golf courses and the pros ate us

Laura Davies tees off at the 1st.

A crowd gathers at the 15th.

out of bananas. And we forgot to thaw the doughnuts one morning so the volunteers had fun cracking their teeth open. Oh and then there was the time we had all the tickets printed in the USA and they came back with no holes or string, so we had to do it all by hand,' she laughs.

Catherine was a founder member of the Ladies European Tour, so she has good experience of how to run a successful tournament. The top 60 players on the Tour receive prize money, which in 1998 totalled £300,000. The winner took £45,000.

Tournament founders Herb Lotman and John Slater both take considerable personal interest in the event, and visit the courses three or four times a year.

'It's hard work,' says Catherine. 'Play starts at 7.00 am and goes on until 9.00 pm, but it's growing and that makes it all worthwhile.'

THE CADDY COMPANY

Richard Cannon is an example of today's professional caddy – smart, business-like and sober! The caddies of yesteryear like Tam the Goose were colourful creatures, but hardly the most reliable of fellows, as Ian Thomson found out in the summer of 1973, when he spent a weekend at The Gleneagles Hotel for a building seminar – with a little golf on the side.

'Our first round of golf was on The Queen's Course,' he remembers, 'and I decided to allow myself the extra luxury of hiring my first ever caddy. I was allocated a tall fellow, who wore a long, ill-fitting raincoat, topped off with a large, flat bonnet.

'He said nothing to me for the first three holes, which I played in my usual indifferent manner – four over par. He then took complete control of the situation. "We shall take a 3-wood this time, sir," he said, and he never let me use my driver again. "We shall aim, not at the marker post, but three yards to the left," and I did. He gave me lines for putts on the double-borrow greens that were unbelievable, but true. As I was about to hit a putt he shouted, "Firm!" and the putt went in. "Don't aim for the flag on this plateau green – we shall aim for that pine tree – yes, that is our line sir." And it was.

'I followed his every instruction. It was magic and I finished with my best ever score. I still have the scorecard! We played our last 15 holes in 6 over par – not bad for a handicap of 20! At the end he said, "Are we playing tomorrow, sir?" I said, "Yes, on The King's Course at 9.00 am." He replied, "I'll be there," and he was, along with 3 other caddies.

'Well, I don't know what happened, perhaps I was suffering the effects of the previous night's "hospitality", but I went from my best ever to my worst ever round. Nothing worked. After a while my caddy stopped giving advice and even stopped speaking to me. The climax came around about the seventh hole, when I asked, "Do you think this is a 7-iron?" To which he replied, "Please yourself!"

'I didn't keep that scorecard! Some time later, it was suggested to me that he might have had a bet on with his fellow caddies that "his man" would win. I had let him down badly.'

Since then, the caddy system has been given more structure and the professional life of the caddy has greatly improved, thanks to the arrival of The Caddy Company, which the hotel employs to manage the caddies.

Richard reports for work at 7.15 am, and when the course opens at 7.30 am he is on his first job of the day. July, August and September are the peak months of the year and Richard has to call upon all his skill and judgement to guide the golfers round the course. 'I have to judge which is the best shot to play, depending on whether the green is uphill or downhill, and what the wind direction is. We also have to judge the best position to aim for from the tree lines, and, once on the green, judge the green lines and predict how far the ball will break. The first shot on The King's is 165 yards, but it is uphill and into the wind so you have to play it as though it were

149

185 yards. Left to their own devices, most golfers will play the ball short. Caddies must cheer the players up and motivate them as well as provide technical guidance. Every golfer is different and has different needs. For me, Nick Faldo is an example of someone with admirable skill and dedication.'

A caddy's day can be long or short, depending on the weather and the number of golfers requiring his or her services. Richard's favourite course is The Queen's Course, which is complex and demands a great deal of precision play.

Although golf is now more of a corporate activity than it was in the 1960s and 1970s, some golfers still like an informal relationship with the caddy. 'It's a question of judgement,' says Richard. 'Some golfers are deadly serious and want extremely precise advice on club selection and green lines. Others are less serious and value a laugh and a chat.'

The weather, of course, can be a quite a hindrance, but Richard doesn't mind the wet. It's very unusual for the course to be closed all day, even in extreme weather conditions, although on the 12th of July 1998 the courses were closed from 10.30 am. This was particularly convenient, as it was the day of the World Cup Final in Paris!

In the old days, before the creation of The Caddy Company, caddies had to bring their own sandwiches and keep warm by burning black rubbish sacks on an open fire. Now there are showers, a locker room, a microwave and central heating. The system is far more professional now, thanks largely to Dave Taylor and Dave McDougall, who set up The Caddy Company in 1995, following talks with Gleneagles Golf Developments. Both men are retired police officers, and were already well acquainted with the golf courses at Gleneagles – Dave McDougall had been chief marshall at the Scottish Open and Dave Taylor was involved in traffic operations at the same event. They were appreciative of the needs of members and guests, and convinced that the caddies needed to be organised on a professional basis.

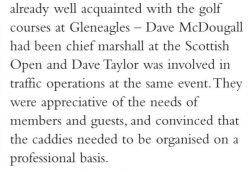

Dave Taylor explains, 'We have 44 caddies, who are all self-employed. We operate a pecking order based on length of service and reliability of the caddy. They should be here 5 days a week, and are well aware that if they are not here, then they may slip down the list.

'The caddies know they can take a day off if they want to, but equally we need to know that we can call on them

DAVE TAYLOR AND DAVE MCDOUGALL

when things get busy in the summer, and for the big tournaments. I remember when we had two big events that clashed, and were five caddies short for half an hour. Sometimes we do cut it a bit fine, and have to wait for caddies to come off the other courses, but all in all it works far more efficiently now than in the pre-Caddy Company days.

'The pay is greatly improved. We charge £28 for a round, of which the caddy gets £23, plus the tip, which is usually forthcoming, as the golfers appreciate the hard work of the caddies. A good caddy will provide the right service for everyone. With a round lasting four and a half hours, a caddy has to be good company, as well as being able to assess the golfer as an individual and respond to his or her needs. For the caddy, there are a few basic rules – don't drink, don't hassle the golfer for more money, and don't look too scruffy. The rest is down to judgement.

The caddies' shelf-life is long. At Gleneagles the youngest caddies are 18 or 19, and the oldest 68, and there is one regular, casual lady caddy who is well respected among the golfers. Not surprisingly, the caddies often form very strong friendships with their regular golfers, who invite them to their homes, send presents and always book them for their games.

A YEAR IN THE LIFE OF A GREENKEEPER

The golf courses at Gleneagles are indisputably among the most beautiful in the world, and it takes a small army of greenkeepers, headed by Stuart Stenhouse and Scott Fenwick, to make sure that The King's, Queen's and Monarch's Courses are always in peak condition.

One man who has witnessed the changes over the years is Scott Walker, who has worked at Gleneagles since just after the Second World War. Mr Walker retired in 1985, but that hasn't kept him away from Gleneagles and he still works part time, keeping his beloved golf courses looking their absolute best.

Scott has always had close connections with Gleneagles. He comes from an Auchterarder family and his uncle was an assistant professional with Gordon

SCOTT WALKER

Lockhart (see page 38). Scott remembers what the courses were like immediately after the end of the war. 'There were sheep grazing on the courses, and that gave us a lot of extra work. During the war, local elderly gentlemen volunteered to keep the courses in a reasonable condition, but there was still a lot to do after the war to get them back to the high standard required.

'Technology has helped us, and we have machines for aeration and spraying. In the early days we relied heavily on horse-drawn cutters.' Scott loves Gleneagles and when we caught up to talk he was fighting a battle with the falling leaves of autumn, to keep the courses clear. He is proud of his job and shows no sign of tiring or wishing to take life at a more relaxed pace.

At the height of summer the Gleneagles greenkeeping army consists of 52 greenkeepers, 2 full-time mechanics (to keep the battalion of grass-cutting vehicles in shape), 3 environmental experts, who look after the fences, trees and wildlife, 1 administrator and 1 full-time tournament organiser, who ensures that The King's Course is in perfect condition for August's McDonalds' Women's PGA Championship of Europe.

The three Gleneagles golf courses are all very different in substance and this calls for particular skills from the greenkeeping staff. The staff are split into two teams: the 'Traditional Team' looks after the 75-year-old King's and Queen's Courses, which are very natural and matured with soil-based greens, while the 'Contemporary Team' cares for the younger Monarch's Course, which has a more modern design with greens that are 95 per cent sand based and which demand a chemical-intensive treatment.

Golf course care is a year-round activity. Stuart Stenhouse describes below what might constitute a typical 'Year in the Life of a Gleneagles Greenkeeper:

JANUARY This is the coldest month, with a lot of frost, and a generous helping of snow. We concentrate on construction work around the course, rebuilding tees, and rebuilding bunkers. The course is still heavily played at this time of year – we only close if there is severe frost or snow.

FEBRUARY This month can be very wet or very cold. More construction work is undertaken, and when the frost eases off, we do essential drainage work.

MARCH There is still no growth on the greens at this time of year, but we will do some mowing to put a stripe on the course for presentation purposes, just to make it look good for the golfers. We often experience what we call a heat spike in March, where temperatures shoot up for four or five days and then snap back into a cold spell during April.

APRIL This is when we start to witness some growth, so there's a rush to lay new turf quickly to allow it to bed down before the new season truly begins. Easter is generally the start of the season. The number of guests at the hotel is rising, so we increase our mowing to make the courses look their best. We try to get the winter rebuilding projects finished by Easter. You can never rule out a bit of snow in April.

MAY We increase the frequency of our cutting to three or four times a week and start top dressing work to smooth off the greens. Reseeding takes place in May, as by now we know the weather will be more reliable. We do some verti-drainage to open up the greens for the summer.

JUNE In June the greenkeeper's workload really does become demanding. Generally, for the next few months we are into an intensive cutting regime, cutting the greens once a day, the fairways, tees and approaches to the greens every other day, and the semi-rough once a week. Our main objective this month is to create a golf course that is neat, tidy and enjoyable for players, so the rough is kept at a reasonable height.

JULY At the end of June and throughout July we begin to prepare for the McDonalds' Women's PGA Championship of Europe on The King's, which takes place in August. We reseed divots on the fairways, smooth bunkers and increase dressings on the greens. We also begin to prepare the driving range for the professionals.

AUGUST This month everything revolves around the McDonalds' Women's PGA Championship of Europe. It's hard work but good fun. Some other courses close down for preparation when they have a professional tournament, but we stay open until the Monday before and open again the following Monday.

While the tournament is being played on The King's, the other courses remain open for general play. The activity really starts three weeks before the start of the championship, when the tented village goes up on the Wee Course and the camera towers are built. After the championship, there is a breakdown period, which lasts another two weeks.

SEPTEMBER Repairs to the courses are completed after the tournament. Large tents tend to kill off the grass beneath them, the stands leave marks and spectator walkways damage the course. We have to work very quickly while we still have heat for growth. This can be an up-and-down month for weather. We might have an Indian summer and need to extend our cutting throughout the month, or it can get cold very quickly and we begin to think about what we are going to do in the winter.

OCTOBER We open the greens up with hollow core and verti-draining to get ready for the rain – the highest rainfall comes in October. We also start to experience our first frost. We begin to seriously tackle the environmental work, pulling up massive banks of broom or gorse, which are invasive plants.

NOVEMBER This is our restructuring period, when we concentrate on re-shaping and re-turfing parts of the course. We get heavier frosts and may well experience some snow during November. We also start to bring in our furniture from the courses – benches, tee-markers, signposts – and rub them down and apply a coat of varnish. It's a good indoor task to get your teeth into when outside is frost and snow.

DECEMBER This is generally a three-week working month, because of the holidays. Christmas is a special time at Gleneagles, and the hotel is full, so we do our utmost to make the courses look good, even though the weather is generally against us – it's always a bit of an anti-climax when you do all the presentation work and then you get six inches of snow. But that's greenkeeping for you. You are always the servant of nature.

THE GOLFING HABITAT

THE GLENEAGLES golf courses are far more than mere sporting grounds; they are also areas of great natural and historical value, so much so that Gleneagles has been designated a 'site of specific scientific interest'.

Kettle holes, large holes filled with organic matter which date from the ice age, are scattered over the courses.

Wildlife observers have a field day on the golf courses. In spring, toads are spawning in the pools and many rare birds are present. In 1997, four female toads were spotted in The Monarch's 10th tee pool and frogspawn in The Monarch's 5th green pool. A blackcap was heard singing by the hotel car park, while mallards and teal are a familiar sight on the nearby lochs. A family of long-eared owls was first seen near Loch-an-Eerie on the evening of the 4th of June 1997, and again on the 10th of June 1997, when seven young were spotted to the South of the Heugh O'Dule on The King's Course.

The area is carefully studied by wildlife experts, who delight in the presence of species and plants that seem to breed in the same place each year. A late breed of red grouse was discovered on The King's Course on the 5th of August 1997 (hopefully they had made a timely exit before the Glorious 12th), and an oystercatcher's nest was spotted on the heath above Loch-an-Eerie, with a family party of common crossbill checking in on the 27th of May 1997.

The Gleneagles golf courses attract an enormous variety of species, and a host of wildlife enthusiasts.

Dragonflies are regular visitors and the highlight of summer 1998 for the wildlife observers was the presence of four common darters in the area. This species, which is traditionally confined to the southern part of Britain, has been spreading rapidly north in the last couple of years and this may be an indicator of climate change.

Technological advancement and the relentless pursuit of the new may have left their mark on Gleneagles, but the enthusiasm for the wildlife and the respect shown for the flora and fauna by the Gleneagles staff prove that the pull of nature is as strong as ever. Provided you are willing to rise at dawn, or stay up all night with a pair of binoculars for company, then you stand a good chance of spotting the usual and the not so usual visitors as they arrive at their preferred breeding grounds.

Gleneagles works very closely with Scotland National Heritage and will continue to do so, to ensure that all wildlife is protected and to enable future generations to study the animals and their habitats and understand how nature lives and works.

Blackcap

CHAPTER SEVEN

This Sporting Life

*Example is the
School of Mankind
And they will
Learn no other*

EDMUND BURKE

HE GLENEAGLES HOTEL started life as a golf hotel, where the leisured classes could while away long summer days playing golf, croquet and indulging in the gentle pursuits that were the preserve of refined society.

The hotel has changed a great deal since then. Since the 1980s, under the visionary leadership of Peter Lederer, Gleneagles has responded to the guests' demand for a more diverse choice of leisure activities.

The famous King's and Queen's golf courses have now been joined by their younger brother, The Monarch's Course. The hotel has branched out into other country sports, with the creation of the Jackie Stewart Shooting, Fishing and Archery schools, The British School of Falconry, The Off Road Driving School, and The Equestrian Centre, while the new, improved Club and Spa have transformed the hotel into the ultimate leisure centre for the new millennium.

THE CLUB

In 1998 a £2.7 million redevelopment programme transformed the Country Club into the spectacular new Club, with facilities that are unrivalled in the UK.

The new Club houses a revamped leisure pool, with a 'volcano' attraction, an outdoor hot pool, a brand-new 20-metre lap pool for the more serious swimmer, and a Jacuzzi to soothe tired muscles after a hard workout. Guests who need to wind down further have the luxury of the relaxation room, the sauna and the steam room. The new Club restaurant is separated from the rest of the facilities by a glass pane, and this creates a unique area in which the

OPPOSITE:

THE SHOOT

Instructors at the Shooting School help a group discover the finer points of clay pigeon shooting.

156

THE CLUB

The magnificent new Club seen from the gardens in the early evening.

members and guests can sit back, read the papers and magazines that are provided and, of course, eat.

The Club's dry sports facilities include the brand-new, state-of-the-art gymnasium with Technogym, which is three times the size of the original one, a dance studio, a snooker room and a squash court. If you hanker after the outdoor life, just take one of the mountain bikes available and head off into the stunning countryside, or hit the jogging trails that are signposted around the golf courses.

The early birds can use The Club from 7.00 am, and the night owls will not be shown the door before 10.00 pm. There is no excuse for not reaching your peak fitness level, as six sports instructors are on hand in the gymnasium to help you attain your targets using Technogym and Cybex equipment.

Claire Birchall is the young, dynamic manager of The Club. Claire thinks that the new Club is precisely in tune with today's lifestyle and fitness requirements. 'We used to have a higher percentage of the older age group, but now that we have the dance studios and crèche (which is free to members), we get a good mix of ages,' she says.

There are two types of membership, a 7-day-week and a 5-day-week, and children have unrestricted access. The under-3s go free, and there is a junior rate for children under 16. The various categories of membership include corporate, student and Spa. Corporate and student membership include free entry to the various classes held throughout the day, such as aquafit and boxercise, and Spa membership allows use of the Spa, hair salon and Club restaurant.

For mothers with young children, the crèche is ideal. Mothers can relax as their children are left in the gentle hands of the Club staff to enjoy the swim clinic, finger painting and hand painting. Nature walks and 'feed the ducks' sessions are popular, as are visits to The Equestrian Centre and the story-reading circles.

Claire feels that the revamped Club attracts visitors and guests to the hotel irrespective of the time of year. 'A lot of people are now coming in winter, to take advantage of the extensive range of indoor activities we offer,' she says. 'I think The Club has attracted new members who will use the other hotel facilities too.'

Mr Bunch, an American gentleman, and his German wife have been active members of The Club since 1990, when they moved from Glasgow to one of the luxurious, new houses near the hotel. Both are well travelled, but Gleneagles remains their favourite spot. 'We wouldn't have made our home here if it weren't for The Gleneagles Hotel,' they say. 'It is the perfect setting in which to spend the rest of our lives. We spend an enormous amount of time at the hotel.'

Both husband and wife play golf. Mr Bunch can usually be found on The King's Course and Mrs Bunch on The Monarch's. Mrs Bunch is a member of the Dun Bracken ladies club, which used to be known as the Dun Dragons by male members a little less than impressed to see ladies on the golf courses. They both swim and use the gym on a regular basis.

Less popular with the Bunches is another hotel regular, Elsie the eagle, who developed the habit of chasing the Bunch's three Burmese cats, Hedi, Hagar and Holly. Elsie also has a keen eye for ashtrays and sandwiches, and used to swoop down on unsuspecting picnickers and terrify the living daylights out of them. Guests and neighbours will be most relieved to know that Elsie has now emigrated to the USA!

Karen Sutherland is another Club member who is prepared to travel from Bridge of Allan, four miles north of Stirling, to Gleneagles in order to use the quality facilities. Karen had moved from Glasgow and was looking for a club with similar facilities to the one she'd left. This was proving difficult, until she came across The Club. 'It has everything I was looking for – a gym, fabulous pools, dance classes and a crèche for my two young children. The boys love coming to The Club, as they are always entertained so well. They go to The Equestrian Centre and The British School of Falconry, and read books and paint in the playroom. The playroom assistants are fantastic and interact wonderfully with the children. The boys love the outdoor hot pool where they can swim even when it's cold.

'I come to The Club on average three or four times a week with the boys. It's great family entertainment and there is a good social life attached to The Club, with the annual ball and the theme nights. It really is an excellent facility,' says Karen.

159

MODERN DINING
The Mediterranean feel of the stylish Club Restaurant.

Baked Feta and Vine Tomato Tart

WITH ROCKET LEAVES AND LEMON OLIVE OIL

8 filo pastry sheets

100 g/4 oz butter, melted

1 tsp sesame seeds

100 ml/3 ¾ fl oz olive oil

zest and juice of 1 lemon

1 clove garlic, crushed

12 vine tomatoes

400 g/14 oz feta cheese

250 g/9 oz packet roquette leaves

salt and black pepper to taste

160

A light, Mediterranean style dish that makes a perfect lunch after a dip in The Club pool. To quench your thirst, Highland Spring mineral water makes a great accompaniment.

❖❖

PREHEAT THE OVEN to 180°C/ 350°F/gas mark 4. Lightly brush 2 filo pastry sheets with a little melted butter, season with salt and pepper and layer them together. Brush with a little more butter and sprinkle with the sesame seeds. Using a round cutter, cut out a 15 cm/7 inch round disc. Repeat with the remaining sheets of filo until you have 4 discs. Place them on a baking sheet and bake in the oven for 5 minutes, until the pastry is light brown and crisp.

To make the topping, warm the olive oil slightly and add the lemon juice, zest and garlic. Keep the mixture warm to infuse.

Slice the vine tomatoes – there is no need to peel or deseed them. Dice the feta

cheese. Layer some tomatoes onto each cooked filo disc, just exposing the edge. Place some diced cheese onto the tomato and season with black pepper. Put back into the oven for a few minutes to warm through.

Lightly toss the roquette leaves with the warm lemon oil. Place the leaves into the centre of each tart, add a touch more pepper and serve.

Serves 4

Good accompaniment:
A light Italian white wine such as Gavi di Gavi or, for a healthy accompaniment, try Highland Spring Mineral Water

THE HIGHLAND SPRING

*A*S WELL as being an area of outstanding natural beauty, The Ochil Hills are the source of the famous Highland Spring natural mineral water. The pure water has long been held in high regard. King James IV of Scotland ordered that celebration ale for his Coronation in 1488 should be made from Blackford Water, which is the source for Highland Spring, and in 1503 King James issued a Royal Charter sanctioning the brewing of 'Blackford beer'.

The prevailing westerly winds carry rain from Greenland across the North Atlantic, which falls in the conserved catchment area in the Ochil Hills. It takes up to 30 years for the water to filter down through the rich mineral-bearing rock strata, before it passes

through a stainless steel pipe and is gently pumped to the surface. The rainfall absorbs the natural minerals as it seeps through thousands of fissures in the layers of rock.

Established in 1979, Highland Spring has grown to become the UK's leading producer of natural mineral water and maintains an extensive conservation area around its boreholes in the Ochil Hills. A ban on farming in the area prevents pesticides, fertilisers or animals from polluting the rainfall as it slowly filters through the rock strata.

People now drink natural mineral water as a accompaniment to food and, of course, it is a must for the Club regular, being low in salts, nitrates and minerals. The Club staff always make sure that guests and members are aware

of the need to replace the fluid lost from the body during a tough work-out or boxercise session, and health professionals recommend drinking at least 1.5 litres of natural mineral water a day, and more if a lot of fluid is lost.

Claire Birchall is strongly in favour of drinking natural mineral water, and drinks it before, during and after exercise. 'It's important to keep the water levels up when exercising,' she says. 'I always sip natural mineral water during my session, and then drink a considerable amount at the end of my programme. It helps the digestive system and keeps skin healthy and glowing.'

Highland Spring is an important member of the local community and supports many activities, including the Gleneagles Festival Day.

THE SPA

THE SPA
*For the world weary, what
better respite than relaxing
in the Spa.*

The Spa is the health and beauty salon built at Gleneagles in 1990 and designed by Champneys. In 1996, the hotel took back the management of the Spa and installed Lorna Campbell as manager.

The Spa is the only salon in the area to offer Shiseido treatments, and Lorna has also developed a new, three-hour long treatment for the face and body which is the ultimate in relaxation and rejuvenation. Two particular Shiseido treatments, the 'deluxe yasuragi' and the 'deluxe shiaku' are guaranteed to relax even the most stressed-out executive. The 'deluxe yasuragi' combines the art of scalp and body massage with Eastern spiritual thinking to create a feeling of natural harmony, while soothing and nourishing the skin. The 'deluxe shiaku' has been designed to encourage the body's natural elimination of fluids and toxins. It begins with a body exfoliation to enhance the absorption of the massage oils, followed by an overall body massage to stimulate circulation and and improve lymphatic drainage.

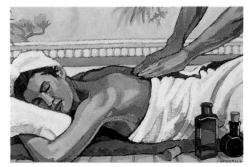

Unlike a lot of beauty salons, the Spa actively encourages men to have treatments, and there is a range of facials, scalp treatments, and massages available which have been specifically designed with men in mind. One of these is the popular 'flight reviver' – guaranteed to give a lift after that tedious long-haul flight. 'We want to offer our clients, guests and Club members a full range of services,' says Lorna. 'We cater for teenagers and pregnant women, and hope to bring in new Shiseido treatments in the near future, as we believe they really are the best all-round beauty treatments available.'

Clair Bain is the hairdressing manager and her team specialise in scalp massage, long hair revival and treatments for thinning hair.

Lorna feels the future is rosy for the Spa. 'The health and beauty industry is a huge one and people are happy to spend time on treatments. People are returning to natural therapies and at the moment, the most popular are the hands-on treatments, such as the aromatherapy massage in the old steam rooms. I think everyone now realises that it is sensible to invest time and money on looking good, not just to improve appearance, but for the future health benefits it brings.'

THE GOLF ACADEMY

'Golfers are increasingly aware of the value of tuition and The Golf Academy at Gleneagles is the centre of excellence for the teaching of golf in Scotland. Our philosophy is that golf should be fun, and whether your aim is to win the Open or just improve your handicap, fun in golf comes from playing to the best of your ability.'

GREG SCHOFIELD
Gleneagles Head Golf Professional

Gleneagles Head Golf Professional Greg Schofield believes golfers must be able to study their own technique. The Golf Academy has been created with the aim of showing the golfers how they *actually* play, rather than how they *believe* they play.

Since its inception, there has been a huge demand for use of this exceptional facility. In less than half a decade it has developed from being little more than a practice ground into the most comprehensive tuition centre in Europe, with an Aladdin's Cave of the most sophisticated equipment imaginable.

Greg, his four teaching professionals and three trainees are able to provide assistance to any golfer, from the complete beginner who has never held a club before, to players of the very highest standard.

Some people are blessed with natural co-ordination, and once they have been taught how to hold the club correctly, the tutor can build on a swing almost immediately. It can take as little as two or three lessons for beginners to get a feel for what they are doing. Of course, playing on a golf course requires training in how to manage the course – playing out of the rough, coping with the bunkers, and putting on a variety of different types of greens.

The first thing you see when you approach The Golf Academy is the traditional practice range, 320 yards long and 150 yards wide, with 15 Astroturf bays. Players who want to use grass tees can be accommodated at the opposite end of the range. The Golf Academy houses a number of individual practice areas which are designed to focus the player's attention on particular areas of his or her game.

165

THE SHORT GAME AREA

When people think of golf at Gleneagles they usually think of The King's, The Queen's and The Monarch's, but par 3 golf has an important place at Gleneagles too. In addition to the relaxing pitch and putt course, Gleneagles has the classy par 3 layout known as the Wee Course, with holes which vary from 123 yards to 213 yards. Little surprise, then, that the Academy houses Europe's leading specialist facility dedicated to the improvement of the short game.

The philosophy of the short game area is simple – golfers of whatever standard can save a few shots per round on the main courses by sharpening up their short game. In recognition of this, three practice greens have been built. Considerable dedication has gone into the construction of the practice greens. All the greens have properly created bunkers and golfers can play a range of shots from various positions. There are also four covered bays from which to play to the greens.

The short game area has its own social calendar too. Target golf competitions have been held there on warm summer evenings – for beginners and experts – accompanied by cocktails, canapés and champagne.

THE SIDE STUDIOS

The side studios are two remarkable rooms crammed full of the latest technology and designed to improve every golfer's game. They enable close analysis of the swing, and have proved extremely popular. Beginners and experienced professionals alike can improve their game through visual learning.

THE GOLF ACADEMY
As every golfer knows, practice really does make perfect.

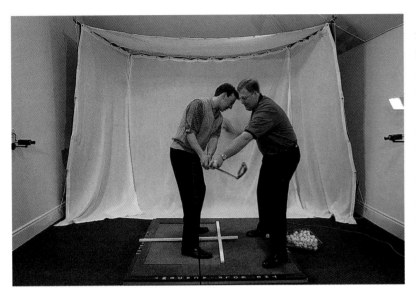

TEACHING
BY CAMERA
Greg Schofield takes a
pupil through his paces.

166

The first studio has four cameras fixed at different points. The golfer stands in the middle of the studio and takes up position. The first camera is on the side wall, four feet away from and facing the golfer. It shows the address position. The second is fixed to the other side wall and takes shots of the golfer from behind. It shows spine movement and gives a good visual impression of the transference of weight as the golfer makes the swing. The third camera is fixed to the ceiling and is ideal for showing if there is too little or too much movement. The fourth camera, which is the one most in use, is positioned 15 feet behind the golfer and shows the plane of the swing, which is what usually determines in which direction the ball will travel. The images from the cameras are fed into a video recorder. The instructor and pupil then study the results together and work out where changes need to be made.

This new visual approach is of enormous help to the golf instructor, who can in seconds highlight and illustrate a fault and let the pupil see where his or her mistakes lie. The studio also has a small, flat practice putting area around 15 feet in length, which is used to help the golfer get a feel for correct handling of the putter and develop the pendulum swing to ensure that the ball is hit smoothly.

The second studio has all the facilities of the first but in addition boasts a 'weight transference platform', which is a very sophisticated piece of equipment, designed to judge one of the most crucial elements in the golf swing – transference of weight. Right-handed golfers need to transfer weight to the right as they begin the backswing and to the left when the ball is hit and during follow through. Golf professionals say correct weight transference is one of the most difficult things to teach, and this is where the platform, with its video display, comes in.

As the golfer stands on the platform, with the ball in front of him, the monitor shows two percentage figures which reveal where the weight is concentrated. The percentage on the left of the monitor shows the proportion of weight through the left foot, and the percentage on the right of the monitor shows the proportion through the right foot. At address, the two figures should be equal. As the golfer begins the backswing, the figures should change so that the vast majority of weight is concentrated through the right foot. As the swing unfolds and the golf ball is driven away, the figures should change so that the greatest proportion of weight is now through the left foot. The figures are then recorded on a video and the golfer can see instantly where he or she is going wrong.

The equipment provides an instant visual record of technique. The Golf Academy can put on video precisely what happened in the lesson for the golfer to keep as a souvenir and reference tool. Still photographs from the video show even more graphically the difference between the old and improved swing.

Terry Venables, one of the world's greatest football coaches, was highly impressed when he visited The Golf Academy during a stay at Gleneagles. 'I was fascinated by how much intricate detail you could see on the videos,' he said. 'I feel this is an area we could look into in football coaching. With this system we could improve the players' body movements when doing set pieces, particularly with corners and free kicks. I think we could make a study using graphics on the video and work out how to increase accuracy and speed. I would love to take some time working with the golf professionals to further understand the system, and its full range of services. Then I'd like to adapt it to the football coaching world, and see if we can produce a similar system to help players reach their true potential.'

THE LONG GAME AREA

Once the swing has been honed in the studios, it's out into one of the six covered bays to put theory into practice. The long game area also has four cameras, which can be hand held or rested on tripods, and which record videos for later analysis. This area has full-length mirrors positioned at all angles so the golfer can see where the problems lie. Sometimes three different angles need to be studied. The instructor will not always accompany the golfer in the long game area – this is the golfer's chance to build on what has been learnt from observation of the video images, and practise the new elements that have been built into the swing until the new, improved technique feels completely natural. The long game area allows golfers to experiment with some of the difficult lies they may face on the course, a particular feature of the undulating Gleneagles courses. A sloping mat, which resembles a discus circle (one side is 10 inches higher than the other), helps the golfer learn how to play from uphill and downhill lies.

THE REPAIR ROOM

Now that woods have metal heads and materials are stronger, golf clubs need less attention. Golfers are also likely to change their clubs more frequently, as they try to keep up with the latest technology. Golf club manufacturers are forever updating their equipment and they invest heavily in research programmes.

One piece of equipment that is still regularly used is the 'loft and lie machine'. The loft of a golf club is the angle between the club face and the ground, which for a 5-iron is typically between 28 and 30 degrees. Individual golfers often prefer to have different angles of loft, particularly on short-distance clubs like wedges, and the machine is able to adjust to take such preferences into account. The lie of a golf club is the angle between the hosel and the ground. A tall person will need a fairly upright lie, a shorter person a flatter lie.

167

168

**A CLOSE EYE
ON THE TARGET**
*Chris Jenkins, Manager
of the Shooting School,
instructs a guest as a
target is released from the
specially constructed, radio-
controlled traps.*

THE JACKIE STEWART SHOOTING SCHOOL

'Always to be the best and to be distinguished above the rest.'

HOMER

The Jackie Stewart Shooting School was opened in 1985 by one of Scotland's most famous sons. Jackie Stewart may be best known for winning the Formula One World Championship three times, but he is also one of the most talented clay pigeon shots in the world, winning the British, Scottish, Welsh, Irish and English championships before he began his full-time motor racing career. Jackie is indeed a remarkable man. His eye for detail and capacity for sheer hard work is legendary.

Jackie Stewart and Gleneagles are clearly a match made in heaven. Both have a desire for excellence and an innate ability to influence and charm, making guests feel like old friends in a special home. And both appreciate the value of good men and women to run their businesses. Jackie Stewart employs the best people for the job, and together his men and women have built up a business that has a first-class international reputation. The School attracts a great deal of corporate business.

Chris Jenkins is the manager of the Shooting School. Chris has a military background and is experienced in all forms of shooting. He works with Noel and

Alan Jones, who are directors of the School. The Perthshire countryside within which Gleneagles lies is the natural home to all of the wildlife represented by the sporting clays in the 13 shooting disciplines, offering the best form of shooting in an ideal environment. There is a challenge for every standard of shot in the 13 shooting disciplines:

1   The Crossing Pigeon.
2   The Driven Grouse.
3   The Gleneagles Pheasant – not a culinary delight from The Strathearn, but a pair of pheasants of intermediate height.
4   The Springing Teal – there are two traps, one more difficult than the other.
5   The Bolting Rabbit.
6   The Running Hare.
7   The Compact Sporting Layout (a combination of all the shots).
8   The Snipe.
9   The Driven Partridge.
10 The King's Pheasant (set off from a 100 ft tower).
11 The Queen's Pheasant (set off from a 50 ft tower).
12 The Woodcock – a crossing target.
13 The Duck.

169

The School has also developed a discipline in which all targets are interlinked using radio-controlled ball traps, so eliminating all the fixed targets. The aim is to simulate nature as closely as possible, with shots appearing irregularly, with varying force.

I have first-hand experience of the Shooting School, as I was part of the Gleneagles Team that competed during the celebrations to mark the School's tenth anniversary. Having had absolutely no experience, I was somewhat nervous. This, coupled with the fact that it was freezing cold and snowing, did not inspire me with confidence. However, on my first trap, the Bolting Rabbit, I hit the target on three out of five clays. This was due more to the fact that my instructor was brilliant and patient than to any previously undiscovered talent on my part, but I nevertheless felt enthusiastic and keen to develop my shooting ability, thereby proving the Jackie Stewart theory that excellence really does produce excellence (well, nearly...).

CHRIS JENKINS

Not surprisingly, the School is the busiest of its kind in the world, closed only on Christmas Day.

Having served in the army, Chris Jenkins knows all about teamwork and appreciates that being a part of the Shooting School automatically makes him a valuable part of The Gleneagles Hotel. 'We are regarded as part of the hotel team, and, as a team leader, I am invited to take part in many functions and meetings at the hotel. Gleneagles and The Jackie Stewart Shooting School have always operated in unison, which is important for everyone. It makes us feel we are all working towards the same goal,' he says.

JACKIE STEWART

THE TWO BEST-KNOWN Scotsmen in the world are Sean Connery and Jackie Stewart. Both are extraordinary men who have achieved greatness in their lifetimes and also contributed enormously to their communities. Jackie Stewart is not only a first-class businessman and self-made multi-millionaire, but has also raised millions for charity. He was born dyslexic, and has had to work very hard to overcome the embarrassment and difficulties that this brings. Jackie is a supreme example of how an individual can transcend problems and hardship to achieve success and happiness.

Jackie's love affair with Gleneagles, which he first visited as a teenager with his father, has survived the test of time.

'I remember going to The Gleneagles Hotel for lunch and afternoon tea with my father. I was very impressed with its grand appearance and affluent clientele. It had an indoor swimming pool, which was very unusual in those days. It looked like it should have been on a luxury cruise ship.

'Later on I went to play golf there and then, many years later, the hotel approached me to see if we could become involved in some activities together. They were interested in reaching a global market and hoped that Sean Connery and I, being the best-known Scotsmen of that era, might be able to help them.

'It was pretty clear that I couldn't build a racing circuit at the hotel, but as

I shot for Scotland and am also the grandson of a gamekeeper, we decided to build a state-of-the-art shooting school. It was opened in January 1985 and was an immediate success. The Shooting School added another dimension to the hotel and provided the guests with an alternative to golf. International visitors are often unused to the Scottish weather, and could quite easily see the attraction of spending forty-five minutes having a go at a new sport, rather than walking round a golf course in the freezing rain for four or five hours. 'We make it as easy as possible for them by providing them with clothing and guns,' explains Jackie, 'all they have to do is turn up.'

'Gleneagles has organised many special events over the years. In 1995, I spent a magical summer's evening listening to José Carreras, Isobel Rey and the Scottish Symphony Orchestra when they came to give a concert in the hotel grounds. It was an incredible experience.

'Just two weeks later, Gleneagles held the Rolex/Jackie Stewart Celebrity Challenge. This event was probably the most memorable we have organised, and was certainly the most glamorous.

'We raised over £500,000 for charity in one day and an evening, and had a star-studded cast. Even the team of gamekeepers represented the *crème de la crème* of the profession – our four gamekeepers came from Sandringham, Windsor, Gatcombe and Balmoral.'

The famous names competed against each other over nine holes of golf, and then did battle in a clay pigeon shooting competition.

Jackie Stewart had done a marvellous job of bringing everyone together and creating a celebrity list to top all celebrity lists. Only someone with his wealth of connections could have pulled it off. The guests included the Duke of York, Commander Tim Laurence, Captain Mark Phillips, Peter Phillips, the two teenage sons of the late King Hussein of Jordan, the Princess Royal and her daughter, Zara, Sean Connery, Anthony Andrews, Nigel Mansell, Tom Conti, Ian Woosnam, Cheryl Ladd, Chris de Burgh, Kenny Dalglish, Dame Kiri Te Kanawa, Colin Montgomerie, Rod Laver, Alberto Tomba, John Francome, Gavin Hastings and, of course, Jackie Stewart himself.

As he looks towards the next century, Jackie feels that Gleneagles is still very much a part of his life.

'Gleneagles has something very special,' he says, 'a very rare quality, a sense of dignity and style that is difficult to find elsewhere. I think that Peter Lederer, George Graham, and their respective teams, and Ian Ferrier and Jimmy Kidd on the golf side, have all done a truly remarkable job.

'My whole family will be at Gleneagles to celebrate the millennium, and I know that the adults and children alike will have a great time and be entertained in style.'

'The hotel's winning formula is that it offers the best of both worlds – you can be active and go for working-out in the gym, golf, fishing or shooting, or, if you prefer, you can opt for total relaxation and be pampered in the Spa. Standards have risen enormously over the years and now there is something for everyone at Gleneagles.'

Jackie Stewart with Jack Nicklaus and Sean Connery.

Whole Roasted Grouse

WITH BLACK PUDDING AND GRIDDLED GREEN VEGETABLES

500 g/1 lb 2 oz new potatoes

4 sticks celery

1 leek

2 small courgettes

12 baby asparagus tips

8 baby onions

3 tbsp olive oil

50 g/2 oz butter

4 whole grouse (oven-ready)

100 g/4 oz shallots

2 stalks of fresh thyme, chopped

50 ml/1¾ fl oz Madeira

300 ml/½ pint game or beef jus

4 slices of black pudding

salt and pepper to taste

Served as a platter for a dinner party, this dish has a great 'wow' factor. It can be served whole or carved.

PLACE THE NEW potatoes in a pan, cover with salted water and three-quarter cook (10-12 minutes). Drain and refresh under cold water until cool.

While the potatoes are cooking, wash, trim and cut the celery, leek and courgette crossways into 2 cm/¾ inch rounds, at an angle. Leave the asparagus and onions whole. Lightly season the vegetables and brush with the olive oil.

Preheat a griddle pan. Slice the new potatoes lengthways into quarters and fry them with the vegetables on the griddle to create a criss-cross effect. Remove and place onto an oven tray to re-heat later.

Preheat the oven to 200°C/400°F/ gas mark 6. Heat the remaining olive oil and 25 g/1 oz of the butter in a heavy-based frying pan, season the grouse and seal on all sides in the pan. Place in a roasting tray and cook in the oven for about 20 minutes, then leave to rest for approximately 5 minutes.

To make the sauce, peel and finely shred the shallots. Melt the remaining butter in a saucepan, add the shallots and thyme and cover. Cook for about 2 minutes, until just translucent. Add the Madeira and the game or beef jus and bring to the boil. Strain and set aside.

Grill the black pudding on both sides until cooked and crispy, then place on a kitchen towel to drain for a few seconds. While the black puddings are cooking, place the vegetables back into the oven for 2-3 minutes to reheat.

To assemble the dish, place a slice of black pudding in the centre of each plate and arrange some of the vegetables and potatoes around it. Arrange the grouse next to the black pudding. Season the sauce and spoon over and around the vegetables. Serve immediately.

Serves 4

Good accompaniment:
A full-bodied red – Rioja Gran Reserva

FISHING

Catching the evening meal in the fast flowing Scottish waters.

THE JACKIE STEWART FISHING SCHOOL

The latest addition to the Jackie Stewart group of activities is the Fishing School, which was opened in June 1998. Fly-fishing is the purest, most artistic form of fishing. The grace and subtlety required to cast a line are not easily acquired, but once mastered make the craft of fishing an extremely satisfying one. The School teaches the art of selecting the right fly, deciding whether to fish on the surface (dry fly), or sink the fly (wet fly), how to cover just the right spot and how to retrieve in the best way to induce the take.

The Queen Mother is perhaps the most famous admirer of the sport. Fly-fishing does attract its fair share of royalty and celebrities, but is increasingly popular with people from all walks of life. 'Modern technology has made it easier for everyone to enjoy fly-fishing,' says fishing instructor Alastair Philp. 'The old-fashioned 9-foot rods weighed several times the modern carbon fibre equivalent, and nowadays a 9-foot rod will do the job of one of the old 11-foot rods.'

Alastair has been a passionate fisherman since he was a child and now spends his time encouraging others to take up the sport. The Fishing School's activities take place in three lochs – The Laich, Westergreenwells, which is by the ninth tee on The Monarch's Course, and the Pump House. The lochs lie among glorious scenery and are well-stocked with brown and rainbow trout.

There are two basic approaches to trout fishing. You can choose imitative flies, which are designed to simulate the type of food the fish will be likely to go for, or you can use lures or trappers (worms, shrimps, snails, aquatic insects, dragonflies and other insects). To fix the fly to the fishing line the fisherman needs the aid of a leader, as the end of the fly line is too thick to tie to the fly directly.

Beginners will only use one fly, but more experienced fly-fishers can use several, thereby increasing the chance of attracting fish. 'It's a highly intricate skill that brings endless pleasure to many fishermen,' says Alastair. 'People of all ages and all nationalities come to us. Sometimes fishermen experienced in a completely different type of fishing, such as sea fishing, will come along and try fly-fishing and find it is a whole new experience.'

No fisherman should stray too far from the lochs, however. 'We have built a safety zone round the golf course so that the guests don't get hit by golf balls, and the golfers don't get 'fished' by fishermen,' explains Alastair.

175

THE JACKIE STEWART ARCHERY SCHOOL

The Archery School was launched in 1995 and is located close to the Shooting School Shop. The Shooting School instructors are also in charge of the archery. As Chris Jenkins says, 'Our role as archery specialists is to match the people to the equipment – we have a range of 'recurve' target bows made from wood and fibre laminates, which are suitable for all ages, left and right handed. If the physical is not matched correctly to the mechanical, then it will not be possible to perform the sport successfully.'

The traditional 'sport of kings' is increasing in popularity again and members of the British Olympic Archery Team have visited Gleneagles to hold demonstrations, which have been of enormous benefit to the instructors and guests. 'I think people find the challenge of co-ordination and control very stimulating,' says Chris. 'Archery is a sport that requires great concentration and is also a good team-building activity for corporate groups, as it helps to build up individual confidence.'

CO-ORDINATION AND CONTROL
Guests practise the essential art of concentration at the Archery School.

Grilled Salmon Trout

WITH LEEK AND GINGER BOUILLON

1.5 kg/3lb whole salmon trout or 4 x 175 g/6 oz salmon fillets

2 tbsp melted butter

1 tsp fennel seeds

juice of 1 lemon or lime

4 heads small pak choi, washed and trimmed

60 g/2½ oz butter, cut into cubes

1 packet fresh tarragon, stems discarded

For the ginger bouillon

1 large shallot

2.5 cm/1 inch piece of ginger

2 leeks, white part only

25 g/1 oz butter

250 ml/7 fl oz sweet white wine

1 litre/1¾ pints chicken stock

For the horseradish potato

750 g/1 lb 10 oz potatoes

120 ml/4 fl oz olive oil

cream or butter (optional)

3 tsp bottled horseradish

If you are using a whole fish, ask your fishmonger to fillet, scale and remove the pinbones from the salmon for you.

FIRST MAKE the ginger bouillon. Finely chop the shallot, ginger and white of the leek and sweat in a little butter in a covered pan for 3-4 minutes, until soft but not coloured. The green part of the leek is not used and can be saved for stock.

Add the sweet wine and chicken stock and simmer gently for approximately 30 minutes to extract all the flavours from the leeks. Sieve and reduce the bouillon to leave approximately 400 ml/14 fl oz.

To make the horseradish potato, peel and boil the potatoes until cooked, then drain. Mash them, drizzle in the olive oil while beating. (If preferred, add cream and butter to make the mixture even richer.) Stir the horseradish into the mashed potato.

Preheat the grill. Cut the salmon trout into 8 equal-sized pieces. Brush the salmon with the melted butter, sprinkle with fennel seeds and squeeze over a little lemon or lime juice. Grill the fish lightly for 2 minutes on each side until just cooked.

To assemble the dish, reheat the bouillon and place the pak choi in it for approximately 3 minutes to cook. Spoon the potato into the middle of 4 high-lipped plates or bowls. Place the pak choi on top of the mash and the salmon trout on top of this. Stir the butter into the bouillon and, when it has melted, add the tarragon leaves. Spoon a little into each plate.

Serves 4

Good accompaniment:
An Australian white wine –
Wynns Coonawarra Chardonnay

THE OFF ROAD DRIVING SCHOOL

The Off Road Driving School at Gleneagles was opened in 1993. Off road driving is one of the most thrilling sports in the world. It might look impossible to get over the obstacles without either being stuck in two feet of water or ending up

perched on the top of a hillock with a broken axle, but, as we eventually proved, it can be done!

One quite ordinary day in 1998 Richard Close, Land Rover Franchise Director of Lex Retail Group, Fiona Wilson, who runs her own successful publishing and marketing company, and I climbed into a Gleneagles special edition Lex Land Rover Discovery and set off on a trip that took us all back to the magic of childhood. It was Fun with a capital F, and very impressive.

Land Rovers can perform over off road areas with greater flexibility than almost any other 4-wheel drive vehicle. The Lex Land Rover has a split gear box which gives up to 10 gear ratios and therefore has particularly good control over off road grounds. You can ascend and descend at angles up to 45 degrees, and you have a wading depth of 19 inches. It also has more clearance than other types of 4-wheel drive, which means you'd have to be doing something pretty extreme to get stuck. Then again, without the experience, you're likely to get stuck anyway!

We couldn't wait to give it a go.

Off we went over ascents that we thought would tip us over, and through water that made us shut our eyes, waiting for the inevitable sound of the engine

178

OFF ROAD
The angles may be frightening, but the Discovery can cope with the toughest terrain.

spluttering. It never came. The plucky Discovery was still going strong while we clung to our seats and closed our eyes in terror. Richard tried to pretend it was all a breeze, but unfortunately for him, his white knuckles gave him away. The angles are truly frightening. The Discovery was sloping sideways at an angle of about 35 degrees, making us all feel as though we were on one of the most frightening rides at Alton Towers – I defy any man not feel scared. Luckily, we had instructor Sandy Readman and Driving School Manager Steve Ford with us. They soon took charge and showed us what the Land Rover Discovery could really do.

Richard thinks that once people know what the Discovery is capable of, and feel confident handling the car in diverse conditions, then they will have great fun with all the family. Off road driving is the perfect way to see the natural environment at its best. The Discovery enables you to splash your way through the streams and fords to discover parts of the countryside not usually seen by a motor vehicle. There's nothing like a picnic at the bottom of a steep glen in the Highlands to give you the feeling you really are at one with nature.

180

*Showjumpers perfect their
art during a training
session in the riding ring.*

THE EQUESTRIAN CENTRE

The Equestrian Centre was the second new facility to be built at Gleneagles,
following quickly on the heels of the Shooting School. It was quite clear that an
opportunity for local people and hotel guests to develop their riding skills in the
beautiful Highlands would be welcomed. It was equally clear that the only person
who would be able to undertake the design and development of such an important
project would be Captain Mark Phillips, one of Britain's most successful horsemen.

Mark first starting riding in pony clubs as a child, and when he left school he
was picked to be a reserve rider for the British team in the 1968 Olympics. It was
the start of a meteoric rise. Four years later he won a team gold medal at the
1972 Olympics in Munich, followed by a team silver medal at the 1988 Olympics
in Seoul. He has enjoyed considerable success in domestic events, winning the
Badminton trials four times and the Burleigh trials once. Few people are more
knowledgeable about the design and construction of equestrian courses.

Mark first became involved with Gleneagles in 1985.

'I had been friends with Jackie Stewart for
many years,' explains Mark. 'At the opening of the
Shooting School in 1985 I said jokingly to Jackie,
"What next then, an equestrian centre?" About a
year or so later Peter Tyrie, the then Managing
Director of Gleneagles, and Peter Lederer, who
was General Manager, contacted me and we
began discussions on the building of The
Equestrian Centre.'

The initial design was for a smallish building, available to hotel guests only. There would be six to eight horses, with an instructor and a groom. However, when Guinness took over the management of the hotel in 1985, they decided to invest in an equestrian centre that would be a true showpiece for Scotland, able to hold international televised events in all riding disciplines. The five-star hotel would have a five-star equestrian centre, with five-star horses.

The Centre has hosted some highly successful events, including a fundraising day for the British Equestrian Olympic team. Mark Phillips often brings his own horses to the Centre to give lecture demonstrations.

Captain Phillips' objective in setting up the Centre was, 'to make riding fun for all levels of rider, from beginner through to advanced, and for all disciplines – dressage, showjumping, cross-country, driving, polo, side-saddle, disabled riding etc. And that is what The Equestrian Centre has achieved. Beginners feel just as much at home as advanced riders, as they are able to use the horses with a quieter temperament and learn their skills in the riding ring on some of the gentler hacks.

Gleneagles has a special place in Captain Phillips' heart. 'I would sometimes be taken to Gleneagles when I was riding in Scotland, years before I got involved in The Equestrian Centre. I was always struck by what a fantastic place it was – very grand and really quite overwhelming. It has a special aura and atmosphere. Staying there is never a too much of a trial!'

For the first five years following his retirement from active competition in 1988 Captain Phillips ran the Centre as his own business. In 1993, he sold out his interest in the management company to the hotel, who now run it as part of their resort. He still maintains close contact with the Centre, however, and returns three times a year to run teaching clinics. As an internationally renowned horseman and coach to the United States Equestrian Team, Mark Phillips is an extremely busy man. He acts as a consultant on various event management and cross-country course design projects, but he always makes sure he reserves some time to visit The Equestrian Centre at Gleneagles.

Although Mark Phillips himself was very young when he began his riding career, clinching his first Badminton victory on his favourite horse, Columbus, in 1974, he feels that it is never too late to start learning to ride. 'Obviously, as with any sport, it is easier to learn when you are young, but I believe that if you start later on in life you can still get great pleasure from riding.'

Diana Zajda is the present manager of The Equestrian Centre. She is assisted by six full-time and a handful of part-time instructors, together with about a dozen students who are all in training for British Horse Society exams. Diana feels privileged to work in the luxurious setting of the Centre. 'I've never seen anywhere finished to such a high standard,' she says.

181

DIANA ZAJDA

'Usually, riding staff spend their time wading through mud and fighting with the saddles and bridles for office space in the tack room. Here we have a pine-lined, heated indoor school and fabulous facilities for both horses and staff. I wouldn't want to work anywhere else.'

Both Diana and Captain Phillips are delighted with the success of the Centre's schools programme, which was implemented to encourage children from local schools to get involved in equestrian activities. The schools get a lot of enjoyment from learning new skills like grooming and looking after the saddle and tack, as well as the actual riding lessons.

The Centre hosts over 100 shows a year. The two most important, senior showjumping events are the three-day Spring Festival in April, and the pre-Olympia event in December. In addition, there are qualifiers for the Royal International and for the Horse of the Year Show, and teaching clinics led by high-level professionals such as William Micklem, Carl Hester and, of course, Captain Mark Phillips.

The range of riding events held at the Centre continues to expand. Junior jumping shows are very popular, and 120 ponies are stabled on site for such events. More and more privately owned ponies are kept in the stables, which is good for the local community, and there has been an increase in the more unusual events, such as vaulting, which Diana describes as 'aerobics on horseback'.

Some of the Centre's horses are real characters. 'We took in Oscar, who is a miniature Shetland,' says Diana. 'He was being kept in someone's back garden, as they thought he'd make a good lawn mower. He was covered in lice and just crying out to be rescued. He was wild when we got him, but now he's really well behaved and a great pony to have in the stable. Arthur is another Shetland, given to us because he kept biting his riders. Then we have Horace, who we call the great escapologist, as he manages to break free at least once a day.'

THE BRITISH SCHOOL OF FALCONRY

Drive out of the Shooting School, cross over the road and you will find The British School of Falconry, housed in a long, low building amongst the moors and glens that provide a perfect setting for this wonderful sport.

The British School of Falconry was opened in 1992 by world-renowned falconers, Emma and Steve Ford. Emma first fell in love with the birds as a child, when one day she looked over a fence and came face-to-face with a magnificent

falcon. By the age of eight she had trained an eagle. From that moment, Emma knew she was destined to work with birds of prey for the rest of her life.

Emma runs The British School of Falconry with her husband, Steve, a horseman and fellow falconry enthusiast, whom she first met at the age of 14. It has been a very successful partnership. Steve and Emma run not only The British School of Falconry. Steve runs The Off Road Driving School at Gleneagles, and together they manage the Land Rover driving school at the

Equinox hotel in Vermont, in the USA. 'It was love at first sight when I met Steve,' says Emma. 'A man who rode Andalusian horses and let a kestrel sleep at the bottom of his bed was clearly the one for me.'

They married when Emma was 17 and Steve 22, partly because they were offered jobs in Abu Dhabi, and had to be married to qualify for work under Abu Dhabi's conditions of employment. However, when British television screened the controversial programme, 'Death of a Princess', the offer was withdrawn and the Fords stayed in Britain. They pooled their resources, had a think about where they were going, and set up The British School of Falconry.

Emma and Steve were introduced to Gleneagles by friends, and their first foray into running falconry there came in 1989, when they organised a special-interest falconry break in the hotel grounds. 'Falconry was becoming very popular,' says Steve. 'We were based in Kent at the time and, after doing the commute from Kent to Scotland a few times, we decided to move the hawks and ourselves up to Scotland permanently. We set up a full-time branch of The British School of Falconry on the spot where the golf driving range used to be.

STEVE AND
EMMA FORD

183

'We opened in April 1992 and have never looked back. The School was such an immediate success that we had to double its size within 18 months. The School can hold up to 22 birds. We actually have 40 birds, 18 of which we keep at home, and rotate with the others, depending on which birds are moulting. The only day we are closed is Christmas Day.'

When Emma starred as the subject of a BBC documentary, 'Countrywoman', the exposure it gave her opened up doors and led to other projects. One of these was the Off Road Driving School at Gleneagles, which is run by Steve. The Fords were also able to open up the US branch of The British School of Falconry at the Equinox Hotel in Vermont, in 1995.

They are both proud to be based at Gleneagles. 'The Gleneagles mentality is very pro-active,' says Steve. 'If you have a good idea then Gleneagles will give you all the support necessary to make it happen. Guests are becoming more interested in falconry, and taking the eagles into cocktail parties is always a great icebreaker. The birds are quite happy to sit and be the centre of attention for a while.'

'Falconry has been my passion for 28 years,' confesses Emma. 'I still dream about it and it fills my every waking moment. Even when the day is cold and wet and I'm trampling over the moors with a bird, I still think I'd rather be doing that than anything else. It is the perfect combination of work and personal pleasure.'

Steve shares her passion but finds the first few days of hunting tough. Although the sport now runs all year round, there is still a peak period during summer and autumn. 'In July we get the birds out of the aviary and try to get back into the rhythm of hard work,' he says. 'We have fat dogs, fat falcons and a fat falconer, all hoping to get fit by the 12th of August – the Glorious 12th! But I have achieved my dream – all I ever wanted to do in life was hunt with peregrine falcons at red grouse over English pointers. That to me is heaven!'

Now that Steve and Emma divide their time between the UK and the US, Debbie Knight has taken over the day-to-day management of the School.

Like Emma, Debbie's love of falconry was awakened at an early age. With a falconry centre on her doorstep in Hampshire, Debbie soon developed a passion for the sport and joined the local club. She read up, took several courses and, finally, got her own bird – a magnificent Ferruginoos buzzard with the rather unlikely name of Reg (named after the person who helped Debbie develop her passion for falconry). Reg is now housed in luxury (by bird standards) accommodation at the School, along with the hawks, eagles, and falcons.

As we take a walk along the gravel path to visit the birds, it becomes clear that Debbie is a woman who rarely takes the easy option. Reg is certainly a challenge. The Ferruginoos buzzard has a reputation for being difficult to train. It is not the most brilliant of hunters in the wild and demands a lot of time and effort from its handler before it is won over. But like most things in life, hard work brings a greater sense of achievement. The satisfaction Debbie felt when Reg finally placed his trust in her was far greater than if he had been a pushover, and now they go hunting together whenever Debbie has the time.

The School is open in the morning and afternoon, closing around 5.30 pm in summer and when darkness falls in winter. Like most of us, the birds need an annual holiday, especially when they start to moult. But unlike most of us, the lucky birds have four months' vacation. In the wild, moulting takes place in spring or summer. In captivity, it tends to be in the winter, as this is when the birds are idle and are particularly well fed.

With this kind of lifestyle, it's hardly surprising that the average age of a bird at the School is twice that of its brother or sister in the wild. The falcons will live to the age of between 15 and 20 in captivity, compared with just 7 in the wild. Harris' Hawks will live to 25 years in captivity and only 7 to 10 in the wild. Gilbert, the oldest Harris' Hawk at the School, is a slightly arthritic old gentleman of 18, who is enjoying his retirement.

The Harris' Hawk has a remarkable character and will live and hunt in groups in the wild. It is good with small children or nervous adults, and hunts rabbits, pheasant, ducks, crows and small animals. Training the birds requires great understanding and patience. Unlike dogs, birds do not display an unshakeable loyalty to their

THE AUTHOR
*Jane Nottage takes time
from writing to meet one
of the birds at the
Falconry School.*

184

owners, but operate on the simple premise that whoever gives them food is a friend. Once they have built up trust in that friend, they will return to him or her again and again, knowing that sustenance is on the way, although, naturally, even the most trusted friend cannot just march up to the bird and snatch its dinner away without offering a substitute. One dish sure to go down well with the Harris' Hawk is an ounce of chicken, which at Gleneagles is given in the form of a cockerel chick, an egg by-product.

When I arrived at the School on a wet and windy August day, I found falconers Ian Smith and Crispin Hill out training a young, seven-week-old falcon. The falcon is more nervous than the Harris' Hawk and tends to catch other birds in flight, rather than swoop down to snatch small animals on the ground. The falconer swings a leather pad called a lure, which represents the particular bird or animal to be caught, and the bird dives at the lure a few times before the keeper allows it to 'catch'. It is necessary to build up the bird's fitness before it can be used as part of the display team, which isn't as easy as it appears, as the birds will only hunt when they are at the right weight. Too satisfied and they have no desire to hunt, too lean and they will not have the strength. The perfect hunting weight of each bird is calculated by the trainers, and the birds are weighed daily.

Both trainers are pleased with the performance of the young falcon. It isn't easy for young birds to work in windy conditions, since they become confused by the different scents in the wind and can get swept away. This was always a particular problem for one Gleneagles resident, a tawny eagle called Elsie. An eagle's eyesight is eight times stronger than that of a human, and its hearing is far better too. Eagles live to the age of about 15 in the wild, and 30 or 40 in captivity. Yet eagles are also lazy, and in this Elsie was no different to her brothers and sisters. However much encouragement she was given, Elsie would only go for the lure. Anything that really moved was instantly dismissed. Her main fetish was catching black dustbin bags, which she loved. Until one day a wind caught her and she disappeared. A frantic search ensued. Eventually a phone call came in from the police in Auchterarder. 'Had the School lost an eagle?' One had been found in Auchterarder.

A new addition at the falconry school is Tarragon, a Russian Steppe Eagle. It is larger than a tawny and smaller than a golden eagle. As I said goodbye to Debbie and made my way back to the hotel, Tarragon was sitting on a perch outside the School looking quite relaxed and happy, and showing every sign of being an excellent addition to the family.

FALCONRY

185

The unspoken bond between human and bird is put to the test during a day's hunting in the glens.

The Millennium

*D*URING A LIFETIME there are a few special moments when the clock stops ticking and we sit back and reflect on what has passed, and on what is to come. The millennium will be such a moment, where the world will pause as one era slips into the next. A new dawn means new opportunities and the advent of the third millennium is sure to bring with it a whole host of hopes and expectations.

To reflect this historic moment, The Gleneagles Hotel will be celebrating with an unrivalled four-day Hogmanay event that will be rich in joy and variety. Each day will be packed with special activities and entertainment for adults and children alike. The Hogmanay festival is destined to become another classic Gleneagles memory, certain to leave the participants with a warm glow and the precious feeling of being part of a much-loved family.

Rupert Spurgeon, Events Manager, gives a foretaste of a Hogmanay never to be forgotten.

THE GLENEAGLES MILLENNIUM

We are creating a millennium maze by planting over 4,000 yew trees in the grounds,' says Rupert. 'We want this maze to be a centrepiece to delight guests as they arrive at the hotel. A time capsule will be put into the maze, so that guests can see what life was like at the end of the second millennium. It really is an incredibly exciting project.

'Over the four days our aim is to give the whole family a truly amazing experience. We are planning to show classic black and white films in the Orchil room, hold Scottish dance lessons to prepare guests for the reels and jigs, and conduct hawking, shooting, fishing and floodlit golf sessions. Then there's the after-dinner games, tarot reading and astrology, and the Casino. A number of prize-winning photographers will be here to take family portraits, and naturally there will be sumptuous banquets and glittering balls with various themes and styles of music.

For the night of the 31st of December 1999 itself we are planning a truly spectacular night of entertainment. The guests will never forget that they spent the millennium Hogmanay at The Gleneagles Hotel.

LOOKING AHEAD
The millennium provides the perfect opportunity for Gleneagles to reflect upon what it has achieved so far, and to think about what the future can bring.

Rupert Spurgeon's life is intrinsically linked to that of the hotel and it is fitting that he should be spending the millennium party right at the centre of the action. His wife works as a beauty therapist at the hotel, his brother was married at Gleneagles, and four-year-old Laura, the eldest of his two daughters, was christened there.

Rupert is enthusiastic and excited, as well he might be. The four days from Wednesday the 28th of December 1999 to Sunday the 1st of January 2000

CHAMPAGNE RECEPTION
Whatever changes are ahead, Gleneagles is sure to retain its special aura of opulence and glamour.

promise to be simply awe-inspiring. Guests will leave with copies of videos and photo albums, so that their children and grandchildren will be able to see how this special Hogmanay was celebrated.

Gleneagles 2000 will become an exclusive club of people destined to be linked forever by their presence at the best party in the world.

A NEW ERA

When the last champagne corked has popped, and the last of the party lights been switched off, what, then, will the future hold? How will the leisure industry change and develop over the coming years and how will The Gleneagles Hotel adapt to the new era? The staff have their own vision of what life could be like at Gleneagles 2000:

Peter Lederer has one simple objective: 'I'd like The Gleneagles Hotel to be recognised as the finest resort hotel in the world, in terms of customer feedback, people and profitability.'

If he were granted three wishes for himself, Peter would like firstly more time to read, secondly, a long family holiday to compensate for the one he had to cancel in 1998 and thirdly, the opportunity to discover the more remote parts of Scotland in his TVR sports car.

Head of Marketing Terry Waldron has been at the hotel for six years and during that time has seen many changes and new developments. 'The staff play a more important role now compared to six years ago. Peter has brought about a shift in the relationships between management, staff and guests, with the result that the staff who actually interface with the guests on the ground have been given real responsibility and the capacity to act upon it.

'There's a greater emphasis on families and the needs of young children. We have created a 5-a-side football pitch because a guest remarked that his children didn't like to play on the grass at Gleneagles, as it was so beautiful and carefully manicured by the greenkeepers. So we decided to set up a special pitch for them and now everyone is happy.'

Terry also has three wishes for the new era: 'I'd like my computer to not only react to my voice commands, but also think for me, so it can store the details of anyone I need to contact in its memory bank and remind me to call them! Naturally, I'd like this to extend to my home, and have a kind of slave who would return my videos, run my bath and, above all, do my aerobics classes for me. What bliss that would be! I would also like to see my nephews and nieces achieve all their dreams.'

Public Relations Manager Margaret Ellis, who has been at the hotel since 1982, has seen many changes, but one thing has remained constant. 'Whatever changes have been made, the return rate of guests remains high. Once they've stayed here they always want to come back to us,' she says. 'I think that even though new technology has changed people's lives, we have used it to enhance the service we provide, rather than let the technology take us over. This means we retain the same human touch and warm welcome that have always characterised Gleneagles. People feel at home and feel that we always have time for them, and that is vital in an age when time has become such a scarce commodity.'

General Manager George Graham is considering expansion. 'We are thinking of adding another wing. This would be a major development as it would affect the whole infrastructure of the hotel, but having the capacity to entertain and feed another 100 people in comfort and style is really what we are aiming for.'

George is also pleased with the way the staff have taken on more responsibility. 'We have created our £500 spending ceiling, which allows any member of staff to spend up to £500 to sort out a problem. By giving our staff responsibility we are also giving them confidence.'

If we take a look into the crystal ball we can visualise how things might change in the leisure industry over the coming years. Terry questions whether there will still be hotels and travel as we know it, or will people simply press a button, Doctor Who style, and arrive instantly at their desired destination? She believes the euro currency will make it easier to compare prices across Europe, and that perhaps one day there will even be a unified currency across the whole world.

Peter Lederer anticipates changes in the education field: 'I think there will be five school terms in the UK, and I think people will take shorter but more frequent holidays, with one long break of a month or so, when they will travel extensively. Stress is sure to remain a constant presence in people's daily lives and this means that there will be a greater need to get away, and more demand for service and value.'

Above all, the Gleneagles staff are looking forward to the challenges of the next century, one in which the demands for excellence, service and entertainment will be greater than ever before, and where the capacity to provide such high standards of service will depend upon the imaginative flair and creativity of every member of staff involved. As George Graham says, 'I embrace the next century very positively. We are looking forward to welcoming both old friends and new to The Gleneagles Hotel.'

189

Index

Acknowledgements

The author and publisher would like to thank the following for their kind permission to reproduce photographs:
Mary Evans Picture Library pages 10, 34, 106, **Phil Sheldon Golf Picture Library** page 62, **PA News** page 69,
Bill McFarlan page 73, **Dr & Mrs McPherson** page 82, **United Distillers & Vintners,** p100-101, 104, **Brian Morgan**
page 126, **GPL/Phil Inglis** page 148, **David Tipling** page 154, **Highland Spring** page 162, **Sporting Pictures UK Ltd**
page 170, **Macintosh Red** page 187.

Special thanks also to **Catriona & Paul McCann** and **Lt Colonel Ron Smith** for supplying the wedding photographs for pages
112-113; **Mary Noble** for the pics on pages 44, 52, 53 and **Jim Lawson** for the photograph on page 38.